ATOMIC WOMEN

The Untold Stories of the Scientists Who Helped Create the Nuclear Bomb

ROSEANNE MONTILLO

LITTLE, BROWN AND COMPANY

New York   Boston

Little, Brown and Company
Hachette Book Group
1290 Avenue of the Americas, New York, NY 10104
Visit us at LBYR.com

First Edition: May 2020

Little, Brown and Company is a division of Hachette Book Group, Inc.
The Little, Brown name and logo are trademarks of
Hachette Book Group, Inc.

The publisher is not responsible for websites (or their content)
that are not owned by the publisher.

Photographs on pages 221 and 222 courtesy of the Emilio Segrè Visual
Archives. Photographs on pages 223–226 courtesy of the Los Alamos
Historical Society.

Library of Congress Cataloging-in-Publication Data
Names: Montillo, Roseanne, author.
Title: Atomic women : the untold stories of the scientists who helped
create the nuclear bomb / Roseanne Montillo.
Description: New York : Little, Brown and Company, [2020] | Includes
bibliographical references and index.
Identifiers: LCCN 2018050922| ISBN 9780316489591 (hardcover) |
ISBN 9780316489584 (ebook) | ISBN 9780316489614
(library edition ebook)
Subjects: LCSH: Women physicists—United States—Biography. |
Nuclear engineers—United States—Biography. | Nuclear
physics—Research—United States—History—20th century. |
Nuclear weapons—United States—History—20th century.
Classification: LCC QC15 .M56 2019 | DDC 355.8/2511909252—dc23
LC record available at https://lccn.loc.gov/2018050922

ISBNs: 978-0-316-48959-1 (hardcover), 978-0-316-48958-4 (ebook)

Printed in the United States of America

LSC-C

10 9 8 7 6 5 4 3 2 1

**To the unsung female scientists
throughout the ages**

CONTENTS

PROLOGUE

July 15, 1945, New Mexico

I n a cabin on the grounds of Harry Miller's Tourist Court, in the town of Carrizozo, Elizabeth "Diz" Graves and her husband, Al Graves, were busy setting up their equipment. Intertwining wires of various colors crisscrossed the room, and odd contraptions with several buttons to press sat atop window sills, along with timers ready to buzz, all to monitor the level of radiation that was about to drift in from the test area. "The Gadget," as the test bomb was originally known, had been brought to an isolated desert spot in New Mexico known as Jornada del Muerto, Spanish for "Journey of the Dead Man," a name many people would eventually find very appropriate. The secret mission, and the Gadget itself, had been code-named "Trinity," referencing a poem by the famous English poet John Donne.

Diz and Al Graves had also lugged to the cabin a seismograph (an instrument to measure the ground's vibrations), a Geiger counter (a type of particle detector to measure emissions during a nuclear blast), a shortwave radio (a type of long-range radio transmission that allowed Diz and Al to hear signals from a distance), and a portable electric generator. The man who'd rented them the cabin had found it all very strange, this young couple dragging along so much unusual equipment, and asked out loud if they planned to blow up the area. Diz and Al hadn't answered him but merely smiled—a private joke passing between them, one the man would never understand. They went on to tell the owner that they would stay just two nights, as they were driving across the country and were only stopping for a short rest. The owner must have thought it odd that a heavily pregnant woman would be driving so many miles in the heat, for any reason at all. But he didn't say anything and he didn't require any further explanations.

On entering the cabin, Al had spread their gear on the floor and atop one side of the bed, leaving a portion of it empty in case Diz needed or wanted to lie down, although he didn't think she would take advantage of a rest.

Diz was now a little over seven months pregnant and, suddenly worried that the radiation would hurt the unborn child, had asked her superiors for an assignment some distance away from the test site. Compared with the experiments she'd undertaken before, this project was the most dangerous of them all.

Her husband had supported her decision, although he had been surprised by her request to be away from the main site. When he'd met her during his graduate studies, such a thing as a little radiation would not have bothered her. Her fearlessness and drive were the two character traits that had appealed to him more than anything else about her personality. She had also possessed a bit of a gruff exterior that dared anyone to tell her how things ought to be done or to disagree with her. That's why he found it odd to see her so skittish, so concerned about the outcome of the experiment, though he knew it was because of the baby.

As he unpacked his equipment in the cabin, Al watched his wife walk up and down the room, either worried about the blast or because the baby was moving wildly inside her. Diz was excited, and while she knew that she was still some weeks away from delivery, she hoped the pressure she felt wouldn't induce contractions.

The cabin in Harry Miller's Tourist Court had a window facing west toward the test site, and on its sill Al had propped the Geiger counter. They checked all the instruments, and as darkness cloaked the area they began to listen over the shortwave to the voices coming from the test area. Hours later, they heard the countdown, and they began to whisper along with it as it inched forward. During the last seconds, the shortwave radio failed, and the voice faded away. Diz continued to count on her own, keeping track.

Although the test site was nearly thirty miles away, they heard the blast clearly, and Diz Graves knew that the bomb had gone off. All her worries and questions would now be answered. The radioactive fallout brought along by the wind did not reach them until some hours later, and by the afternoon, Diz was alarmed to see the readings on the Geiger counter as its needle swung to the right. As more hours passed, the needle on the counter shot all the way off the scale. Al shared his wife's concerns and he decided to telephone base camp to see what the scientists were doing. He was informed that General Leslie Groves and various members of the military were trying to figure out whether or not the area's residents needed to be evacuated, but while Al was on the phone, he learned that they had decided against evacuation. Diz continued to take readings, her mind eased by the fact that by late evening the radiation levels had tapered off. Al made a quick telephone call to the officials to let them know the latest developments.

Despite their eagerness to complete the project, Al and Diz Graves, like many in the scientific community, had come to suspect that they were leaning over the edge of the unknown and were afraid of what they would discover there. While the bomb was being constructed, they had wondered what truly would happen if and when it exploded. Would it actually work? What would the outcome be if it did?

They had joined the others in Los Alamos because they feared that the Second World War would last for several more years, that Adolf Hitler would be the first to build the bomb and unleash it on the rest of the world, and that every other country would have to pay the consequences. They had, in a sense, asked no questions about the validity of their work; they had not wondered about the lives of the innocents who would be caught in the middle of the conflict or whether they should have built the bomb just because they had the means to. It had seemed to them that what they were doing was justified, the only course of action they could have taken to save their lives and the lives of others.

But being pregnant and feeling the child growing inside her had changed Diz's and Al's ideas somewhat. What would the bomb let loose? Diz had asked her husband one night when she was unable to sleep. What would their child and the children of others inherit? How would the blast, if successful, be seen by the world at large? Those were their questions as they'd waited in the cabin for the bomb to go off. Now they would get their answers.

Not too far from the cabin where Diz and Al Graves had set up their apparatus, Diz's younger coworker, Joan Hinton, huddled under a blanket, trying to protect herself from the rain that night. Joan was shaking, not only because she was cold and jittery, but also because she was feeling angry and, in a strange way, profoundly offended. She hadn't been officially invited onto the test area to view the explosion, and she didn't know why. Unafraid, she had decided to see it anyway. She deserved to, she had told herself over and over as she left the dormitory; given all that she had contributed to the bomb's construction, she deserved to see it.

She had given the officials plenty of time to change their minds, but the invitation hadn't arrived, so Joan had asked for the help of a friend who also worked for the Manhattan Project—a research and development project undertaken by the United States during World War II to produce the first atomic bomb—and who happened to own a motorcycle. Off Joan and her friend went, riding wildly to the site as they tried to dodge government jeeps. When they arrived, they met another couple who also had wanted to view the blast, and together they quietly sneaked inside the perimeter while it was still dark and waited for the countdown. They settled on a hill some fifteen miles away from the official detonation area; in spite of the distance, they knew they would get a very clear view of the explosion.

The air seemed bitterly cold to Joan, even though it was July. Deep darkness engulfed them, but they could not light any matches or portable flashlights, as they feared being discovered by the authorities. It took a few moments to get accustomed to the surroundings, but when they did, Joan's eyes could distinguish the slopes of the mountains, the hills around her, and the fine blades of grass that swayed in the breeze. Up above, a thick layer of clouds covered the sky, and there were no stars flickering that evening, no moon to guide their view.

She was aware that the test was going to happen some-time that night, but then the hour passed and nothing happened. Looking up, she knew that the rain was to blame. She scanned the sky and the hills, wondering what would happen if the test did not go ahead as planned, what failure would do to her coworkers, to the scientists and engineers who had been working nonstop for months.

But then, at 5:30 AM, it came. They noticed an astounding ball of light cutting through the sky and felt the heat coming toward them as the bomb went off. Joan and her friends felt a blast shake the ground. It was a ripple at first, then a more powerful and erratic tremor beneath them, the earth shaking and rumbling as if protesting. "It was like being at the bottom of an ocean of light. We were bathed in it from all directions. The light withdrew into the bomb as if the bomb sucked it up. Then it turned purple and blue and went up and up and up," she said later.

"We were still talking in whispers when the cloud reached the level where it was struck by the rising sunlight so it cleared out the natural clouds," she went on. "We saw a cloud that was dark and red at the bottom and daylight on the top. Then suddenly the sound reached us. It was very sharp and rumbled and all the mountains were rumbling with it. We suddenly started talking out loud and felt exposed to the whole world."

Everything was suddenly illuminated, and where darkness had been a few minutes earlier, she could now see clearly for miles around. The mountains, the hills, the sky, the grass, the stunned faces of her friends—everything was aglow. There was a moment of pride when she reflected on what she had contributed to the project, and also a moment of apprehension for precisely the same reason. But, regardless of how she felt, one thing was true: The atomic age had just arrived.

Sitting at a desk in her laboratory in Washington, DC, Dr. Elizabeth Rona was interrupted by an assistant who brought in a telegram. She reached out and unsealed the envelope, then looked up at the clock affixed to the wall: It was early morning, before classes started. All around her were tubes and microscopes and bubbling gases; the essence of her work. Here, in the United States, she had tried to replicate the laboratories in which she had worked in Europe, but it seemed to her that something was always missing. She didn't know precisely what.

The air all around her seemed to vibrate. She remembered the time months earlier when she had received a similar telegram, also marked RESTRICTED, inviting her to help in a secret effort to end the war, asking her to offer her expertise on plutonium. And, intrigued by the possibility, she had accepted without hesitation.

Today, it appeared as if that expertise had come to fruition. The bomb had exploded, the telegram said. The test
in New Mexico had been a success. And she had not even
been invited to view the explosion. But it didn't matter to
her whether or not she had witnessed it; what mattered was
that the Americans had succeeded first. At that moment,
she thought of her friends and relatives still stuck in Europe
and the innocent people caught in the middle. What would
happen to them?

PART

ONE

A European
Beginning

chapter one

All That Glitters

arie Curie slowly slid into bed and looked at the small tube resting on her night table. It glowed fiercely, bright and shiny, like a most precious jewel. She was fascinated by it, and while she didn't know whether it was necessarily a good idea, she decided to keep it nearby to mark its discovery, which had happened in December of 1898. She and her husband, Pierre Curie, knew that it was a highly radioactive substance, but neither of them believed that such a small amount would cause them any harm. In fact, Pierre himself had snatched a small amount of it from the shed where they worked and now carried it with him at all times, hidden in the pocket of his jacket. It was good luck, he told people. And it was good to feel it there,

to remind him of how far they had come and of how far still they had to go.

Marie and Pierre Curie met in 1894, when Pierre was an instructor at the Municipal School of Industrial Physics and Chemistry in Paris. A friend of Marie had made the introduction, thinking the two might hit it off. Marie was twenty-six years old, and Pierre was thirty-five and studying the properties of magnetism. Pierre and his brother had also been involved in designing manual instruments, such as scales, one of which later became known as the Curie scale.

Pierre and Marie quickly found themselves in a passionate relationship, based as much on emotions as on their shared love of science. The union developed fast, as they were alike in many respects: They lived for science; they hardly ate anything all day; and they suffered from intense bouts of insomnia. Even if sleep overcame them, at some point each awoke with a start, as if feeling guilty for sleeping when they could have been doing something more productive. Neither Pierre nor Marie was very good with people, particularly when deeply involved in a project. They were single-mindedly devoted to science, and everything else they deemed a nuisance.

Pierre had insisted on marrying Marie almost from the moment he met her, but she refused. She was not French, and she wanted to return to her native country of Poland to teach and continue her research. It was only when Pierre assured her that he would be willing to give up his life, his work, his family, and everything else that was meaningful to him in Paris to go with her to Poland that she said yes. Only a man who truly loved her and wanted to be with her would have promised something like that, she reasoned.

While she had been in Paris for years, Marie always thought of Poland as home. She was born Maria Sklodowska in Warsaw, the fifth and last child of Wladyslaw Sklodowski and Bronislawa Sklodowska (née Boguska), both well-known professionals. Her father was a professor of physics and mathematics, and her mother was a principal at a private school for girls until Maria's birth.

From a young age, Maria Sklodowska had been an excellent student, and her father provided her with additional learning opportunities that she did not have at her school. But while initially she seemed to thrive on the demanding schedule that she imposed on herself and that her father helped her sustain, the reality was that the pressure she felt eventually led to a handful of physical breakdowns, which she continued to suffer from as she grew older.

But her devotion to knowledge continued, and it did not surprise anyone when she graduated from high school at the age of fifteen, earning top standing in all her subjects. She intended to continue her studies, but given that the area they were living in was ruled by Russia, girls were not allowed to attend university. Maria came up with a plan.

She made a pact with her older sister, Bronislawa, known as Bronia: Maria would find work as a governess and help Bronia through her medical studies in Paris. When Bronia finished school and became a doctor, Maria would then move to Paris and live with her, and in turn Bronia would repay the favor and help Maria attend university and follow in her path.

It had seemed like a perfect plan. And so Maria took a position with a wealthy family in the Polish countryside, where she met and became involved with the family's oldest son. It was with him that she experienced passion for the first time. But when his family learned of the affair, they refused them permission to marry, in view of their different social status. While their relationship continued unbeknownst to his family for some time, it eventually ended when she realized that she could never marry him.

When Maria's work contract ended, Bronia tried to persuade her to move to Paris, where she could keep her end of the bargain. Instead, Maria decided to stay in Poland. With her father's help, she was assigned laboratory space in a museum, where she began to replicate experiments that she had read about in several papers devoted to physics and chemistry that her father had given her.

She stayed in Poland for a year, refining her experiments and her research skills. But she now found herself with some money in hand, and she finally decided to travel to Paris. She stayed with her sister for a while, but Bronia had married and was pregnant. Finding that she needed more privacy, Maria moved out.

Despite not being fully proficient in French, she had enrolled at the Sorbonne, using the French style of her name, Marie, and continued to excel, graduating in 1893 with a master's degree in physics. Just as she had done in high school, she placed first in her class. Not satisfied with that degree, she earned another degree the following year in mathematics.

It was around this time that she was introduced to Pierre Curie, and their romance moved swiftly. In July 1895 they married in a simple ceremony where they did not even exchange rings and for which Marie chose a simple dress that she could wear afterward in the laboratory.

A little over two years after the wedding, Marie and Pierre Curie's first daughter, Irène, was born. Marie tried raising her daughter herself but realized that she needed outside help. Pierre's father, Eugène, who had lost his wife, didn't mind moving in with them to care for the baby. Life became a little easier for Marie with her father-in-law looking after her daughter as well as taking care of some of the household chores and doing a bit of cooking, skills at which she had never really excelled.

During this time, Marie studied the properties of magnetism. As she delved more deeply into research for her doctoral thesis, something else caught her attention. It had nothing to do with her research, but it intrigued her all the same. She learned of Henri Becquerel's work on uranium salts. Becquerel had noticed that his uranium salts emitted some kind of perplexing invisible rays of energy on their own without exposure to light. Marie Curie was captivated by this discovery and wanted to uncover what those rays were about, to measure them, and, more specifically, to find out why this phenomenon happened. Her detailed experiments allowed her to come up with her own hypothesis: There were traces of another substance in the mineral, and it was more radioactive than any element anyone had ever seen before.

She continued her experiments with more excitement and discovered the existence of two previously unknown elements. In 1898, she identified polonium, which she named as a nod to her native Poland. Mere months later, the second element, radium—named for the Latin word for "ray"—came to light.

Discovering the two elements had not been easy, but now Marie set herself an even more difficult task: proving their existence by isolating and purifying them. In order to start the process of purification, Marie had to get a decent amount of pitchblende, a form of uranium ore now called uraninite. This she dissolved in acid, separating the elements. She had to stir huge pots of boiling solutions with a long iron rod, a process that was strenuous and left her drained. Over and over, she undertook this process, distilling thousands of gallons from the pitchblende, which left her with only enough radium to fill a bottle cap.

That she had managed not only to discover radium but also to isolate it and determine its atomic weight stunned the scientific community.

As if that work to isolate radium weren't hard enough on its own, Marie began working part-time as an instructor at a teacher training college for women in nearby Sèvres, while at the same time she and Pierre continued their experiments. It was trying work that allowed her barely enough time for eating and sleeping. However, she would later recall those days as being the happiest time of her life. Some assumed it was because of the birth of her daughter, but the reality was that Irène had nothing to do with it. It was the hours of working in tandem with Pierre that made her happy, focused on her research in the hopes of another discovery. She would say that this pursuit had given her life meaning.

To only a few friends did she reveal that her mothering duties sometimes kept her away from what she loved to do the most: work in her laboratory. When she could not leave her child with her father-in-law, she brought Irène to the lab and left her in a small crib nearby. In fact, baby Irène was sleeping peacefully when her mother isolated radium, the test tubes glowing bright in her parent's hands.

When people learned that Irène had often been left in her grandfather's care or perhaps didn't receive as much attention from her parents as she should have while Marie and Pierre engaged in their experiments, it was Marie who bore the brunt of the criticism, not Pierre.

What helped Marie to be seen in a better light was the fact that radium could be linked to medical cures. She had dedicated her life to the betterment of humanity, and her detractors eventually agreed. If her daughter had been slightly neglected—which she was not—millions of others benefited from it.

In 1903, the Curies won the Nobel Prize in Physics for their research into radioactivity. They shared the Nobel Prize with Henri Becquerel, who had inspired Marie in her scientific quest. Marie did not know it, but there had been a quiet movement within the French scientific community to prevent her from receiving the Nobel Prize along with Pierre Curie and Henri Becquerel. Despite all that she had accomplished, and all that she had discovered, some still believed that Marie did not deserve the honor.

As it turned out, the Royal Swedish Academy of Sciences had found out about the plot, and a Swedish mathematician had alerted Pierre Curie to the schemes occurring behind their backs. Pierre let it be known that a prize relating to radioactivity could not exclude Marie Curie. Henri Becquerel had inspired her concepts, but Marie had seen them to fruition and had isolated the radioactive elements. How was it possible to exclude her, to deny her the prize and the acclaim that went with it, when she was responsible for everything?

Despite Pierre's imploring and his acknowledgment that she had spearheaded the project and the discoveries, it was widely assumed that Marie had received the prize more because she had assisted Pierre than because she deserved it on her own merits. That belief became blatantly obvious when the Nobel Prize was handed out. The president of the Swedish Academy of Sciences illustrated the couple's success by uttering the proverb "Union is strength." Then he quoted the Bible: "It is not good for Man to be alone; I will make a helpmate." The clear implication was that Marie had served as Pierre's wonderful and faithful assistant during his experimentation.

This was also the time when Marie lost a baby, a little girl who was born too early. Marie always blamed herself for that death. She admitted that she had worked too hard during her pregnancy, particularly in the few months before the birth. She later gave birth to another daughter, Ève, in 1904, which eased her sorrow somewhat.

After Marie Curie received the Nobel Prize, she continued her teaching and research. She didn't know it at the time, but her discoveries would have huge and devastating consequences in the rush to build the atomic bomb. Had she known this, she likely would have not been so eager to open her space to other scientists—especially the many female students—who wanted to learn from her. Their research with their mentor Curie would later make all the difference once World War II started.

chapter two

A Shy and Quiet Girl

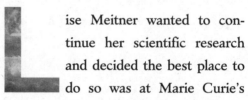ise Meitner wanted to continue her scientific research and decided the best place to do so was at Marie Curie's laboratory in Paris. Lise applied to study with the noted scientist, but she was saddened to read the response letter: Curie had rejected her application to study in her laboratory. Lise Meitner didn't know why. She thought of Marie Curie as the mother of radioactivity and had sent a letter not only expressing her interest in the field but also listing her qualifications, and that she believed she would fit quite nicely in the Parisian laboratory. But Lise had been denied.

Swallowing her disappointment, she continued her life in Vienna. But soon, seeing no future for herself beyond teaching, she decided that attending Max Planck's noted series of lectures in Berlin would be worthwhile. Planck was a noted German physicist, and while he was not her first choice, Lise knew that he would have much to teach her. However, she didn't know whether he would be open to the possibility of having her study with him. She knew that while Planck was not thrilled about women scientists and academics, believing them mainly capable of being mothers and housewives, he sometimes made exceptions. To her surprise, he agreed; he would allow her to attend his lectures at the University of Berlin. Although this was not Lise's original plan, it was a new direction and a new opportunity, so she took it, assuring her parents that she would remain in Berlin for only three months, six at most. She didn't think she would find the environment in Berlin as stimulating as Vienna's, she told them, or the one she would have found in Paris with Marie Curie. However, she needed to give it a go, regardless.

Lise adjusted herself in her seat and felt the train chugging forward and watched the cityscape of Vienna morph into more pastoral surroundings. She thought back to how her journey had started so many years ago, and how her love of physics had brought her to this life-changing moment.

She had entered the kitchen one morning, as she did every morning, to have her usual breakfast. She had found her father sitting at the table, drinking coffee and reading the newspaper before heading to work. He was always very interested in the latest news, and splattered across the pages often were stories of Marie Curie and her husband, Pierre Curie, who had just discovered radium. The papers suggested that one day, radium would be the cure for everything.

Lise did not ask her father what radium was, nor did she bug him for more information about the Curies. Even within her family, she was a shy and quiet girl who had a hunger for books. She would remain that way growing up—though when her notoriety as a scientist grew, her shyness gave way to confidence.

She grew up in a household that thrived on knowledge. Her father, Philipp Meitner, was a prominent lawyer. Her mother, Hedwig, was a homemaker whose parents had paid for her to attend high school—even though public education commonly ended at fourteen for girls in Vienna in the nineteenth century. Nonetheless, Hedwig was a very progressive woman. She had a broad view of politics and history and wide-ranging interests in music and art, which she tried to impart to Lise and her siblings. Hedwig was also the ruler of the house. She taught her eight children to obey their parents, especially their father, as well as to be able to think for themselves.

Despite the fact that her father had a demanding career, it was to him that Lise felt closest. She liked the fact that he had dedicated his life to his profession and that he had learned everything there was to learn about the law. He could debate anyone with respect to the law, in any setting and at any time. She loved to watch him do so.

Lise enjoyed spending hours with him, out in the city, just the two of them, talking about the various monuments and the history behind them. As the years rolled by, these outings with her father took the place of playtime with friends, such as the ones her siblings had, and later on made up for her lack of dates with boyfriends, such as the ones her sisters brought home. While she remained devoted to her studies, she always looked back on her time with her father with great affection.

Growing up in Vienna in the late 1800s, Lise Meitner was a student at the Elevated High School for Girls, but she was unsure of what her future held. She was reserved and, unlike most others her age, did not make much of an effort to attract a husband. Still, she was certain that she did not want to be a part of the "kitchen, children, church" lifestyle that all her schoolmates were striving for. While others considered her unusual, she often stared at them and wondered why they would fall into the role that society had assigned to them.

Since childhood, Lise's true interests had been science and mathematics. Several other girls at her school preferred math and science, too; a most unusual bunch, they often stuck together. From her father, Lise had heard of Madame Curie, and while she had not asked him for further information at the time, she later read about her accomplishments. In her success and in her experiments, Curie had shown that it was possible for a woman to build a life in science.

But if Lise wished to follow in Madame Curie's footsteps, she would need to learn more about mathematics and physics. She knew that she needed to do something drastic, such as attend the University of Vienna. But one problem stood in her way: Only a few women were admitted to the University of Vienna each year, and of those women who had gone there, several had said, "You have to be twice as good as a man to get in!"

Undeterred, Lise worked up the courage to bring up the subject with her father. Surprising even herself, she stood her ground, firmly telling him that she intended to go to the university. She wished to learn all that Madame Curie had learned, and possibly even more. So her father agreed. Not only that, but he paid for a tutor to prepare her for the entrance exam.

Lise and two other young women joined professor Arthur Szarvassy, who helped prepare them for the exam. He was enthusiastic about women's education, so he made it his business, and his mission, to teach them as much as he could about mathematics, chemistry, and physics. And Professor Szarvassy knew a lot. Lise's lessons took her way back to ancient Greece, and she learned about the first man who had conceived of the atom and how that idea had changed the ways of looking at the world.

The university entrance exam was held in a large boys' school. It should have been held in a place attended by both girls and boys, Professor Szarvassy said, but that was the government policy, and they had to go along with it. It did not surprise him that his three pupils felt intimidated. Of

27

the hundreds of people who had shown up to take the test, only fourteen were young women, Lise included; and they came from all over Austria. When they finished the long and arduous exam, they were herded into the corridor to wait for the results. The women glanced at one another with looks of doom on their faces, while the men smirked, heartily believing that they would pass while the women would naturally fail.

Professor Szarvassy came out to meet them, bringing with him the good news: His students had passed the exam.

Lise Meitner enrolled at the university, eager to gain as much knowledge as she could, and she promptly filled her schedule by enrolling in lectures on chemistry, physics, calculus, botany, history, literature, art, and music—as if she couldn't get enough of everything the university had to offer.

In a lecture attended by hundreds of students, she was often the only woman in a sea of men. Their heads would turn as she walked into the room, and they would watch her as she settled into her seat. Quickly enough, she discovered the prevailing attitude drifting through the university hallways: Women could attend the lectures, but they should remain quiet and not ask any questions or intrude on the men's serious business of learning. Women should merely sit, silent and docile, and be grateful that they had been allowed inside the hallowed classrooms.

She learned that most people, teachers and students alike, believed that women and scientific knowledge did not mix.

Age-old customs held that men and women were born with different character traits: Women were good in the home, where they could indulge their natural tendencies for cooking, cleaning, and rearing children. The university and laboratory environments were no place for women, most people thought, believing that women did not have the mental energies or physical strength needed for a life devoted to science. Lise Meitner found it disturbing to come face-to-face with such mentalities sometimes, especially in a university.

She noticed that female students at the school were not so much included as tolerated, while some of the men actually showed downright hostility toward them. That this attitude was present not only among the students but also among the teachers bothered her even more. She often muttered to herself: "It's not fair." Indeed, it was not fair that the women had to prove themselves not only equal but also superior to the men.

In spite of her own frustrations, she persevered and even thrived.

When Ludwig Boltzmann returned to teach at the university the following fall semester after a sabbatical, life changed for Lise Meitner. Professor Boltzmann was a pioneer in thermodynamics. Lise Meitner became determined to take his classes. She wasn't aware of it yet, but he would have a great influence on her life.

She often found herself sitting at his lectures in the Institute for Theoretical Physics, an old run-down apartment building not far from her other classes. She liked Professor Boltzmann; she liked his way of teaching, his enthusiasm, and his innovative theories, which very few others appreciated—and ultimately divided the scientific community. Occasionally, his classes were canceled for what were deemed "personal reasons," which she suspected had to do with his frequent bouts of dark moods. She was sorry then, not only because she found herself with an empty block of time she needed to fill, but also because she despised the idea of her professor suffering.

It was another professor, Franz Exner, who incited Lise's eagerness to take exams for her doctorate. She could be the second woman to earn a PhD in physics from the University of Vienna, he told her one day.

She turned in her dissertation on November 20, 1905, and prepared to wait. Days passed and she heard nothing. She didn't even bump into Professor Exner in the hallways, as she usually did several times a day, in order to gauge his demeanor for a clue as to whether or not she had done well. Paranoia took over, and she became convinced that he was avoiding her so that he wouldn't have to share the terrible news. She resigned herself to the fact that she had failed. Then, on the morning of November 28, she saw Exner rushing toward her with the news that her thesis had been approved. She would now have to sit for two sets of orals, one on December 19 and a more detailed exam to defend her work on December 23. Finally, in February 1906 she was officially awarded her degree. It was an extremely proud moment for Lise and her family.

But her happiness was later marred by a news report she happened to read: Pierre Curie had been run over and killed by a horse-drawn wagon. The newspapers called it a "senseless tragedy."

Although she now held a doctorate, she began work in Professor Boltzmann's laboratory at the university as one of his assistants, alongside another assistant named Stefan Meyer. It was not a terrific job for someone with her qualifications, but it was a first step toward the career she desired, and she enjoyed the work. At the same time, she was also getting her teaching certificate, which was something her father wanted her to do, as there was safety as well as status in a teaching job. But the more she thought about teaching, the more she realized that what she really wanted was to be a scientist and to make a life and a living out of it.

When her first article on radiation was published, she was eager to show it to Professor Boltzmann, and she rushed to his classroom, expecting to find him as she always did, sitting behind his desk. Instead she found only Stefan Meyer, his eyes red and puffy from crying. The professor wasn't there, he told her through mumbled whispers. Exhausted by a recent illness, the professor had requested time to travel to the Italian seaside town of Trieste, where he was to decompress and recharge. He had planned on returning the day before. But something must have happened. Meyer held out a newspaper for her to see. She took it from him and read the news: Professor Boltzmann had killed himself while in Trieste. He must have been overcome by one of his fits of desperation, Meyer said, and gone there in the hope of feeling better.

Lise had a difficult time dealing with the professor's death. He was a strong and intelligent man whom she had admired, and the laboratory was a somber place without him. His presence was everywhere, and his death cast a shadow over the entire staff.

The next spring, a visitor came by the institute. Max Planck—the same professor Lise would seek out after learning that she had not been accepted in Marie Curie's laboratory—was the chair of theoretical physics at the University of Berlin. After Professor Boltzmann's death, Planck received a letter offering him the position at the laboratory.

He decided to visit the lab, eager to talk about the job with Stefan Meyer, who was temporarily in charge, and to tour the facilities. Afterward, he directed his attention to Lise, extending his hand toward her and telling her that he was very happy to shake the hand of a "lady doctor." Like the rest of the staff, Planck was saddened by the death of Professor Boltzmann, a man who had been a huge influence on his life and especially on his work in quantum theory.

Lise was surprised. She had known Professor Boltzmann

for many years, and he had never mentioned Dr. Planck to her. She ventured to tell him of the work she was doing and the paper that would be published in the summer, along with the ones she hoped to publish in the years to come. Professor Boltzmann had been a great influence on her life, too, she told Dr. Planck. Talking to Dr. Planck helped Lise on two levels: It helped her to understand new theories on physics, and it helped ease her mind away from Professor Boltzmann's suicide.

As it turned out, Dr. Planck did not take the job at the institute but returned to his position at the University of Berlin. Lise soon began to think that there was no future for her beyond the laboratory. She knew that she needed to learn more about the new theories in physics, and the only way to do that was to leave Vienna and study abroad.

She made the decision to leave Vienna at the age of twenty-nine. She told her parents that she intended to stay in Berlin about three months, maybe six if she found that she had a lot to learn. But she lived there for more than thirty years.

chapter three

A Life in Learning

J ust as Lise Meitner had, Elizabeth Rona headed to Berlin. She was going to work for Otto Hahn, the director of the Radioactivity Department at the Kaiser Wilhelm Institute for Chemistry. For the past fourteen years, Otto Hahn and Lise Meitner had been working closely together, expanding the world's knowledge of radioactivity. Elizabeth arrived to find a smooth-running department equipped with the latest instruments. The community that surrounded the institute seemed entirely focused on science, something she liked, even if not all the pursuits were geared toward radioactivity.

At the institute, Elizabeth came to know not only Otto very well but also Lise. She knew that Lise was originally

from Vienna, having made her way to Berlin to study under
Max Planck and be assigned to work as a theoretical physicist with Otto Hahn.

Elizabeth Rona was immediately fascinated by the
experiments Lise Meitner was conducting at the time on
beta decay. Lise believed that beta particles, in the same way
as alpha particles, must form an energy field.

Elizabeth liked Lise immediately, even though she found
it hard to get to know her. Lise was quiet and shy, more of
an introvert than Elizabeth had ever been. It took some time
to crack that hard reserve. They were both outsiders who
shared a devotion to science, and their work brought them
together. Elizabeth came to admire Lise's tenacity in solving
scientific challenges; she was like a dog with a bone, one she
never intended to give up.

Lise told Elizabeth that she had always suffered from
horrible stage fright. This did not surprise Elizabeth. Lise
admitted that she dreaded the start of any lecture she
gave; in fact, she tried to avoid giving lectures altogether.
But no one saw a trace of fear on Lise's face when she gave
a talk. Elizabeth attended several of Lise's lectures at the
institute, and found Lise to be an engaging and eloquent
speaker. Elizabeth told her as much, something that Lise
appreciated.

Despite her friendships with Lise and several others
outside the laboratory, Elizabeth found life in Germany as

harsh as it had been back home in Hungary. There was also a particular dislike for women, especially those involved in the sciences. As in Lise Meitner's Austria, women were supposed to live by the motto "kitchen, children, church."

Elizabeth had rented a room in the home of a German couple, both of whom held PhDs in zoology. She thought their mutual backgrounds in the sciences would make for a pleasant interaction. However, it turned out that she was wrong. Despite his wife's credentials, the husband would not allow his spouse to work outside the home, keeping her a virtual maid. And every time he bumped into Elizabeth heading to or returning from the institute, he would glare at her with disdain.

Lise understood what Elizabeth was going through. She had experienced the same situation at the Kaiser Wilhelm Institute for Chemistry, and she hoped life would change for the better for every female scientist.

Elizabeth Rona found that she and Lise Meitner had much in common, including the way each had come to study science and the influence their fathers had on them.

It was the early 1900s, and Elizabeth Rona's family was spending the summer holiday in their house just outside Budapest. As she looked out her bedroom window early in the morning, the birds were singing, the grass was green, and the sun was low on the horizon.

There, sitting beneath a tree, was her father, surrounded by folders, books, and all kinds of correspondence. He was deeply involved in his work, and even when she knocked on her bedroom window to catch his attention, he didn't flinch. She wondered what had him so engaged. Still wearing her pajamas, she went outside. "What can be so interesting that it makes it worthwhile to get up at the crack of dawn?" she asked. He looked up and replied, "Research."

From that day forward, the word *research* took on a mythic significance—an importance she could not explain. She made up her mind that she would also have to find something to research, something that would nudge her awake at dawn with the same eagerness as her father.

Samuel Rona, who was then a well-known dermatologist in Hungary, was happy that his young daughter had developed an interest in the sciences. On her first day of the school year, he brought her to the Holy Shepherd's Hospital in Budapest, where he showed her an X-ray machine, explaining its intricate design and how it worked. Other children later talked of walking to the local pastry shop to commemorate that special first day with fancy pastries and cocoa. Instead, Elizabeth received a scientific lesson on the merits of the X-ray machine and was allowed to have her way with its buttons.

A few days later, Dr. Rona came home in the evening in a very fine humor. He put his briefcase and papers on a nearby table and, without removing his jacket, called Elizabeth to come sit by him, as he had a special surprise for her. With much ceremony, he showed her a small tube that he had been hiding in his pocket. "Radium," he told her. "And someday it will cure skin diseases." He felt that radium would revolutionize the medical world.

She then learned of Marie Curie and her husband, Pierre Curie, who in their Paris laboratory had made the radium discovery. But at that moment, Elizabeth, sitting by her father, could not have imagined that one day she would be a pupil in Madame Curie's laboratory, or that she would come to know Madame Curie as well as she did. Elizabeth would also come to know and learn from Marie Curie's daughter Irène, whose teachings she would take all the way to America.

It was not surprising that Elizabeth, watching her father flourish in his career, would want to follow in his footsteps and become a doctor, too. But she was surprised when he disapproved of her career choice. There were few women doctors, he told her, as it was a tough field for them. Elizabeth would have to choose something different if she desired his approval. She pondered this for a moment. She had chosen medicine not because she particularly liked it, but because she wanted to follow in her father's footsteps. What did she truly want to do? She realized that she liked the study of chemistry better and decided to pursue that.

During Elizabeth's second year at the University of Budapest, her father died. To make matters worse, he had died from the same bacterial infection he had spent countless hours helping others overcome: erysipelas. It seemed that he had been treating an infected patient and, for some unfathomable reason, had neglected to wash his own hands before scratching his head, where a minor scab already existed. An especially nasty case of the infection took root, quickly spread, and killed him.

Elizabeth returned to school with a heavy heart but determined to finish her studies. By the time she was twenty-one, she had received PhDs in chemistry, physics, and geochemistry. Despite all her studies, though, she still felt limited by her knowledge and yearned for more. Several of her friends and classmates had joined the technical Karlsruhe University in Germany, and she decided to follow them, eager to study under Georg Bredig, who at the time was one of the leading physical chemists in Europe.

Most of the professors were stuffy, typical of those she had met before, but Professor Bredig had a warmth that reminded her of her father's. When he invited her and the rest of the class to his house to continue the lessons, she accepted. It was there that Elizabeth met the professor's wife, Rosa, a German cook who refined her skills by feeding the students and indulging in her favorite activity, baking cakes.

While Elizabeth enjoyed those visits, there was one aspect she disliked. She was the only woman in Professor Bredig's laboratory, so when the class was invited to his home, she was shuffled to the parlor or the kitchen with the other women, as they believed that she needed female companionship. This meant she couldn't chat about science with the rest of the class. "The conversations dealt with children, cooking preserves; recipes were exchanged. To these discussions I could not contribute. How I longed to be with my colleagues, to hear and talk shop," she later admitted. No one realized how much she detested those women's conversations, and she did not have the heart to tell them.

But rather than Bredig, it was Kazimierz Fajans who introduced her to the new field of radioactivity. This area of study would take hold of her imagination for many years to come. Professor Fajans, who also invited students to his house, did not discriminate. Women could join the scientific conversations there, and there Elizabeth found herself at home.

She remained at Karlsruhe University for only eight months, studying briefly in London before returning home to Budapest at the outbreak of war in 1914. There she had the opportunity to work with George de Hevesy, who had just completed the first experiments using radioactive tracers to observe chemical processes—a technique that would win him the Nobel Prize almost thirty years later. Elizabeth's interest in radiochemistry was growing, and in Hevesy's lab, she used the radioactive tracers to determine how molecular layers dissolve.

While her scientific work continued, Elizabeth could not completely cut herself off from the world at large. Events around her interfered, particularly in 1919, when the Communists took over Hungary. She later said that her birthday that year was the beginning of the end of her peaceful youth. She was supposed to meet her family at the opera for a celebration but had received a telephone call telling her to go home instead. A group of armed Communists had gone into the opera house and executed a Catholic priest.

More troubles followed. The Communists took over Elizabeth's apartment, leaving her and her mother with the use of only one room. They hid whatever money they had under wood paneling before the officers rummaged through everything they owned, looking for cash and other valuables. Unable to bear the situation, Elizabeth and her mother moved in with an aunt, whose house was already overcrowded. Not only were the living conditions terrible but also food was scarce, and what they could manage to buy was expensive. When money was not available, they had to pay with jewelry or clothing or even small furniture.

The takeover lasted only several months but was followed by a counterrevolution known as the White Terror. The government imprisoned, tortured, and executed anyone suspected of Communist sympathizing. This included leftists, intellectualists, and some of Elizabeth's colleagues. For a time, the laboratory was nearly empty, and she ended up teaching more courses than she thought she could handle. It was then that Otto Hahn, at the Kaiser Wilhelm Institute in Berlin, offered her a research grant and she resigned.

She accepted the grant offer, and from that day forward, the study of radioactivity became her vocation.

After the stint in Berlin, which lasted only months, while summering at an Austrian resort, Elizabeth heard a knock on the door of her bed-and-breakfast just a few days after her arrival. There stood Stefan Meyer, a short, middle-aged man with a wide and engaging smile. Meyer also happened to be the director of the Institute for Radium Research in Vienna.

He had heard that she was in the area and wanted to meet her. It seemed that their interests overlapped, he told her. He asked if she would like to talk and maybe go on a hike in the surrounding countryside. She immediately said yes, and those talks and hikes continued for the rest of the summer. They chatted about science, and they chatted about nature. They talked about the travels they had both enjoyed, all while trying to identify the various types of grass and plants they encountered along the paths. It was a fun, relaxing, and enjoyable time.

Before Meyer left, he asked Elizabeth to join his staff at the Institute for Radium Research. That summer was not only the start of a lovely friendship but also one of the longest job interviews ever conducted. She agreed, happy to have another job in her field.

By the time he met Elizabeth, Meyer was one of the pioneers in the field of radioactivity. At the Institute for Radium Research, he didn't so much engage in new experiments as supervise those of the other scientists. He was looked upon as a master, an expert who was there to inspire and give guidance.

The environment at the institute was inviting. "The atmosphere at the institute was most pleasant," Elizabeth later said. "We were all members of one family. Each took an interest in the research of others, offering help in the experiments and ready to exchange ideas. Friendships developed that have lasted to the present day. The personality of Meyer and that of the associate director, Karl Przibram, had much to do with creating that pleasant atmosphere."

Although by this time Lise Meitner was succeeding in her field and making great advances in the sciences, there were moments when it still irritated her that she had not been allowed entrance to the Curie laboratory in Paris. On the one hand, she felt like a failure; a role model of hers had told her that she was not good enough to participate. On the other hand, those who were eagerly accepted by Madame Curie had arrived on her doorstep, suitcase in hand, unaware of what they were getting themselves into.

Elizabeth Rona arrived in Paris in 1926, sent by the Institute for Radium Research to learn from Irène Curie how to handle polonium sources. Elizabeth immediately made her way to the Left Bank, on the banks of the Seine, where the Curies' laboratory, known as the Radium Institute, was located. Before entering, she walked around the building, catching a glimpse of the backyard garden, where she saw a multitude of plants and blossoms of various colors and heights. She was delighted; she had been told that Madame Curie, and especially her daughter Irène, loved flowers and always made it a point to have a profusion of them around. She also noticed that a balcony on the second floor opened to the garden. She suspected that it was a bedroom, whose occupant's first view of the world upon waking was of the fresh plants and flowers.

Elizabeth was excited to meet the famous Madame Curie but also felt a shiver of apprehension running down her spine. She had a suspicion, one she hoped was unfounded, that like many other people of her stature, Madame Curie would turn out to be a conceited snob who barely spoke to her students.

She entered the institute and met an assistant, who led her to the back of the building, where the laboratory was located. There Elizabeth was surprised by the vision that was Madame Curie, a thin, pale woman in ragged lab coat, walking here and there among her students. This was the image that would forever accompany Elizabeth when she thought of Madame Curie after leaving the institute.

Elizabeth arrived that first day at lunchtime. Right away, Madame Curie let everyone out for a break and walked to meet Elizabeth, asking her if she'd eaten. Elizabeth said that, yes, she'd had lunch prior to arriving. That was good, Marie Curie said, as she hated to waste time on such frivolities. And with that, Marie Curie removed a piece of bread from her lab coat and began to munch on it. Elizabeth was startled. She had imagined that Marie Curie would indulge in a somewhat more elaborate and extended lunch, as most of the French enjoyed doing. But Marie Curie ate only bread while working in the laboratory—always a small piece that she had tucked away earlier. She found stopping for lunch useless. Why waste so much time over a meal when one can be working on an experiment? However, her students disagreed, and they got their lunch break.

Right after lunch, Madame Curie gave her lectures. Elizabeth learned early on that this timing was not the most conducive to learning. The students had just returned from a heavy meal, Madame Curie spoke in a low and steady voice, and the place itself was kept warm, thus many of the students had a hard time following her, and there was a tendency to nap instead. Elizabeth would have done things differently.

Elizabeth noticed that most of those in attendance were

from Poland, and that the majority were women, which she appreciated. Also, as a rule, if there were difficulties or dangerous experiments to be performed, Madame Curie performed those herself rather than allowing one of the students, however advanced, to do it. And Irène was always by her side.

But on one occasion, a few days after Elizabeth's arrival, Madame Curie made an exception, and Elizabeth became a part of that process. No one refused an invitation from Madame Curie, even if Elizabeth had no idea what the experiment was about. Intrigued, she had agreed, and now, here she was, trudging to the lab in the haze of the afternoon.

Madame Curie needed help opening a glass flask containing a very strong solution of radium salt. The flask had been sealed for years, and they both understood that because of the strong radiation, the solvent water had broken down and hydrogen peroxide had accumulated. If they did not take the proper precautions, there could be a very powerful explosion.

Knowing Elizabeth Rona's reputation already, Madame Curie felt that with her help she could avoid the hazard.

However, something went wrong, and a loud explosion rocked the laboratory, one that was heard throughout the institute and the neighborhood, and made the rest of the students snap out of their afternoon reverie and come running to the laboratory.

Madame Curie explained that she had used a file to

scrape away at the lid of the flask, to help the wax around it melt. But the explosion that followed had been so strong that the flask had fallen from her hands and shattered, spreading glass everywhere. Fortunately, neither Madame Curie nor Elizabeth had been hurt or contaminated. Elizabeth then noticed Madame Curie's fingers, whose tips had been burned by too many previous experiments with radioactivity, and blamed that for the lack of dexterity she had just displayed.

In spite of the accident, Elizabeth was happy that she had been invited to work with Madame Curie and that she had the chance to spend some time alone with her. Before arriving in Paris, she had been warned by Stefan Meyer that Madame Curie was a very introverted woman. She liked her privacy, he had told Elizabeth, and kept her distance from people, even from her students.

After that explosion, it seemed that Madame Curie's reserve had broken a bit. She often talked to Elizabeth about her long friendship with Stefan Meyer, who had helped her procure the pitchblende from the mines of Joachimsthal in Czechoslovakia, then part of Austria. It was from that pitchblende that she had first extracted polonium and then radium.

But she also had a more personal reason to feel indebted to Meyer, and that had nothing to do with science, she told Elizabeth. During the recent war, it was Meyer who had kept

Madame Curie updated on the conditions of her family back in Poland. He had also managed to send them food parcels, which allowed them to fend off starvation and survive when many others hadn't. She owed him a debt that went beyond any repayment imaginable.

At the laboratory, Elizabeth watched Irène prepare the polonium sources. Irène had pretty much perfected George de Hevesy's and Friedrich Paneth's technique of separation, which used electrolysis to separate polonium from lead-210 and bismuth-210. Irène used plutonium and gold electrodes and a weak solution of nitric acid. Polonium was then dissolved from the metal and deposited on a silver film, which was rotated in the nitric acid solution. Elizabeth watched Irène use this method over and over, but she could never match Irène's high yields until she later figured out how to increase the concentration of polonium by distilling it.

Elizabeth liked Irène. Although she had been told that Irène could be standoffish, she didn't find her so. She thought Irène was much like her mother, a shy person bent on following her own path rather than the one others had set up for her. She was warm, honest, liked romantic poetry (particularly the French poets), and enjoyed hiking—an activity that was dear to Elizabeth. Irène simply occupied an awkward position at the institute, as there were some who felt that she had gotten her job through nepotism.

Elizabeth also became aware that the Curie laboratory

was highly contaminated. Nonetheless, the situation did not seem to bother anyone, least of all Madame Curie, who worried more about the radium's safety than she did her own.

Elizabeth watched every morning as Catherine Chamié, who would later become her friend, removed the solutions from the safety box and, with a small, creaky cart, brought them into the laboratory. Lead bricks surrounded the cart itself, which was returned to the safe at night. Chamié was the keeper of the radium, and it was her duty to keep watch over it. Only she could go into and out of the safe.

Chamié had developed a paranoid attachment to the radium. Every evening, after she and Elizabeth left the laboratory for their respective boardinghouses, Chamié would stop midway and rush back, sensing that she had neglected to return the radium to the safe. Elizabeth would wait for her by the side of the road, knowing very well that Chamié had performed her job diligently but that no amount of assurance would help. Moments later, the woman would return, as she did every evening, comforted that, indeed, the radium was in its safe place.

Soon Elizabeth returned to Vienna, bringing with her all that the Curies had taught her about polonium. She did not know yet how she would use that knowledge, but some years down the road, the Americans would come calling, wanting to learn all she knew about the radioactive elements. Elizabeth would be very grateful for the time she had spent with the Curies in Paris.

chapter four

Power Couple

1933

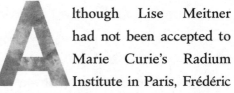lthough Lise Meitner had not been accepted to Marie Curie's Radium Institute in Paris, Frédéric Joliot, a young physicist, had been. Despite his youth, he had already acquired a great reputation, and notable things were expected of him. He had arrived at the lab expecting to learn a lot from Madame Curie. What he had not anticipated was to fall in love with Madame Curie's daughter Irène, who worked in the laboratory with her mother. A year later, they were married, and together they aggressively began to tackle the study on nuclear research. In 1934, they made history when they discovered that elements such as aluminum could be made radioactive when bombarded with radium.

In many ways, Irène Joliot-Curie was like her mother. They liked the same things, they studied the same subjects, and their characters were almost identical. Just like her mother, Irène would go on to win a Nobel Prize, too, but few would remember her name. She sometimes thought she had been cursed with the same notable last name as her parents, though she appreciated that she had been blessed with the talents of them both. Born during the most productive years of her parents' lives, she had received little attention from them, and in fact most remembered her grandfather Eugène during her infancy and childhood.

Irène knew she was not well liked by the majority of those who worked at the institute. Even the women disliked her, which she thought was shameful. She did not like to gossip; whereas for the others it was a hobby. Small talk made her uncomfortable, as it did her mother and, to a lesser degree, her father.

Irène was serious—too serious, some people said. She did not display the carefree attitude that women were supposed to show when in a crowd, smiling and laughing even when one didn't feel like acting that way. She was reflective by nature, and if she found a situation humorless, her face and attitude reflected her feelings.

She was also not a fanatic about her appearance, especially since she spent most of her days in the laboratory. Did one need to dress up or paint one's face as if attending a performance at the theater in order to delve into a scientific experiment? She didn't think so. But others saw her disregard for convention as arrogance.

Sometimes she recalled her youth as a series of adventures with her sister, Ève, swimming, cycling, and walking for long stretches of time in order to toughen up their bodies and dispositions, something her parents and grandfather had desired in both children.

Irène had also learned early on that, unlike in other families, where siblings competed to get their parents' attention, in the Curies' household it wasn't with Ève that Irène had to fight to get noticed; it was with the laboratory. It was in the laboratory that her parents spent most of their time, and, it seemed to her, it was in the laboratory that they always preferred to be. So instead of loathing and begrudging the place, she had learned to love it, for it was there that she could be with both her parents, especially her mother.

Although few gave Irène the same credit bestowed on her mother, it was she who would bring scientists closer to developing the atomic bomb with the discovery of artificial radioactivity in 1933.

In October 1933, Irène and Frédéric Joliot-Curie took part in the Solvay Conference in Physics in Brussels, Belgium. Held every few years, the invitation-only conference brought together the best minds of the world's scientific community to discuss a single topic. That year the topic was the atomic nucleus. Among the invited participants was a cluster of brilliance: Madame Curie, of course, along with Niels Bohr, Enrico Fermi, and Lise Meitner.

Irène and Frédéric took to the stage and began relaying the results of their experiments. They spoke of neutrons and positrons that were emitted at the same time, and they spoke of the properties of the nucleus. As they talked, they could hear a rumbling in the audience, and members of the conference began shifting uncomfortably in their seats. Heated conversations soon ensued.

Oddly enough, one of those who seemed passionately opposed to the Joliot-Curies' ideas was Lise Meitner, who had arrived from Berlin with a notable reputation for meticulous research. Lise told the Joliot-Curies that their results must be wrong: She had undertaken similar experiments herself and found not a single neutron. It was the wrong attitude, of course, coming from a scientist who should have known better: Simply because she had not arrived at the same conclusions as the Joliot-Curies did not automatically make them wrong. Yet Lise continued to badger the Joliot-Curies, especially Irène. She almost never spoke up with such passion in her laboratory or in front of her colleagues and associates, most of whom were men. Those who knew her later surmised that in speaking to Irène, she was speaking to her equal, to a woman, and was thus capable of letting loose. There was no need to watch her language, no need to be careful about her thoughts and ideas, and, to a certain degree, whether her judgments had been entirely correct did not matter. For better or worse, Irène took the brunt of Lise's wrath.

Lise Meitner's arguments deeply depressed Irène and, to a lesser extent, Frédéric. Still, they continued their studies in Paris, and in early 1934, they released the first reports on their discovery of artificial radioactivity. It did not surprise them that the reports were met with a good deal of skepticism, especially from Niels Bohr, who was quick to dismiss Irène. "In a letter from Mme. Joliot, she says she thinks that she has evidence of electron emission under the influence of alpha particles on beryllium," he wrote, adding, "but I suspect that the beta particles tricks on their photographs are due to Compton effects on the atoms of the wall of the cloud chamber." The Compton effect was then explained as the scattering of a photon, also known as an elementary particle, by a charged particle, usually an electron, which resulted in a decrease in energy.

Soon Irène and Frédéric were invited to Vienna, where Stefan Meyer was able to hear firsthand lectures they gave about their discoveries. Irène and Frédéric Joliot-Curie were thrilled to be receiving some professional recognition, although it was coming during a turbulent time in their lives: Marie Curie was extremely ill. It seemed that all those years of exposing herself to the effects of radium had finally caught up with her.

By early 1934, Irène and Frédéric Joliot-Curie were bombarding aluminum with alpha particles. Irène had often heard the story of her parents finally seeing the radium late one night while she slept peacefully in her crib. There was something romantic about it that appealed to her nature, and often, as she worked into the wee hours of the night with Frédéric, she wondered whether something like that might happen to them, too. She did not have to wonder for long. One night in January, something extraordinary occurred. After bombarding aluminum with alpha particles, they were finally able to remove the source of the alpha particles. They made the announcement that they had achieved artificial radioactivity.

In late January, the scientist Enrico Fermi was returning to Rome following a vacation. The break had allowed him to spend the Christmas and New Year's holidays with his family, away from his laboratory. It had also wiped away some of the disappointment he had felt when the journal *Nature* rejected the article he had submitted on the theory of beta decay. Although he had published a similar article in two other journals already, the failure to publish this particular one had stung him badly. A proud man, he saw any failure in his work as a fault in his character. But now, back in Rome and trying to catch up on his work, he read about the Joliot-Curies' discoveries in an area he had been studying for many months. He felt inspired and wondered whether neutrons would induce a similar reaction in an atom's nucleus.

Fermi and his team in Rome bombarded elements with neutrons, proceeding down the periodic table to uranium. Neutrons did indeed create minor reactions in an atom's nucleus, but with uranium, the team couldn't identify the new radioactive substances that were created. Fermi did not recognize that he had actually split the atom's nucleus—a phenomenon Lise Meitner would explain later, with worldwide repercussions.

On July 4, 1934, in Paris, Marie Curie died. She would not see her daughter and son-in-law win the Nobel Prize in Chemistry in 1935 for their discovery of artificially induced radioactivity.

By then, scientists in Europe and the United States were using the Joliot-Curies' technique to try to understand Fermi's results—most scientists thought he had created new elements heavier than uranium. Only one dared to think differently.

Ida Noddack, a German scientist who was working in a government laboratory in Berlin, reviewed Fermi's reports and criticized his chemistry in an article in September 1934. She believed he had created not new elements but rather isotopes of uranium, chemically identical to the element but with a different number of neutrons. It was conceivable, she wrote, that uranium's heavy nucleus had shattered into several larger fragments. Although Noddack had co-discovered the element rhenium in 1925, she was neither a radiochemist nor a nuclear physicist. Her idea did not fit with what was known about nuclear reaction at the time. No one paid it any attention.

At the Kaiser Wilhelm Institute for Chemistry in Berlin, physicist Lise Meitner convinced chemist Otto Hahn to start their own experiments bombarding uranium. They bombarded it with fast neutrons and slow neutrons, for short times and long times, all the while filtering out the new radioactive substances to study. They were convinced new elements were being created, but Lise still had trouble explaining the physics of the nuclear reaction that led to them.

Irène Joliot-Curie and her husband then tried a different tack in Paris. Along with their lab partner, the young Serbian scientist Pavle Savić, they studied the radioactive substances without chemically separating them first. They saw all the substances that the Berlin team had identified plus one other, with a surprisingly strong radioactivity of 3.5 hours. Later, when they did the separation, they found the 3.5-hour substance in the filtrate left over from separating the others. Irène and Savić presented their findings in 1937, suggesting that the new substance was an isotope of the element thorium.

The Berlin team couldn't believe they had missed something and thought Irène and Savić's technique was flawed. They went looking for thorium in the filtrate and couldn't find it, concluding that the intense radioactivity must have been due to contamination. But Irène and Savić continued to reproduce and study the 3.5-hour substance. They found its chemical behavior was entirely different from the other radioactive substances. Again the Berlin team dismissed their findings, with Hahn calling the 3.5-hour substance "cusiosum." In September 1938, Irène and Savić published the details of their experiments. Reading them, Fritz Strassmann, the third member of the Berlin team, realized that Irène and Savić were indeed on to something. He repeated their experiments with his own methods of separation. The results prompted Lise and Hahn to reconsider their ideas and investigate further.

What the Berlin team would find changed the world.

chapter five

In Exile

1938

In 1938, Lise Meitner was spending her first Christmas holiday in Sweden. With her was her nephew Otto Robert Frisch, a scientist himself. She was excited to have him for company. The two shared similar interests and were alike in many aspects of their personality; he was one of the few family members with whom she could talk science. She didn't like Sweden, with its icy-cold temperatures and the wetness and dreariness to which she awoke every morning— everything seemed duller to her, grayer than it had been in Berlin, and uglier than it had been in her native Vienna.

She also felt isolated, far away from home, from family and friends and colleagues, although she was happy to be alive and with people she knew. The only good thing about Sweden was the mail service. With a two-day delivery between Stockholm and Berlin, she could send letters to her longtime collaborator Otto Hahn and her other colleagues and feel as if she were still working with her old friends and had a finger on what was happening in the scientific world.

Frisch had arrived a day earlier than expected, eager to surprise his aunt. He knew she felt lonely in Sweden. She had become used to a certain lifestyle in Berlin, and even after several months, she was still unable to acclimate herself to her new surroundings. He knew that she would appreciate a visit from him and some familiar discussions.

He had always been impressed by his aunt and enjoyed his conversations with her. Whereas his aunt was a quiet and thoughtful woman—some would even say somber—Frisch was bright-eyed and eager, a friendly man who put everyone at ease. He had been working in Copenhagen at the Institute of Theoretical Physics under Niels Bohr, a job he enjoyed and a place he felt at home.

Lise knew Bohr very well. She first met him in 1920, when he visited Berlin to speak at the famous Wednesday colloquium. Not fully understanding his lecture, Lise and the younger physicists had invited him to lunch without the older professors. Bohr was charismatic and friendly, spending hours answering questions. She met him again a year or two later, when Bohr had invited her to Copenhagen to lecture at his new Institute for Theoretical Physics. Combining theory and experiments, Lise and Bohr had a similar approach to science, and they clicked. They talked "about everything under the sun," and formed a lifelong friendship, strengthened by her regular return over the years to participate in Bohr's renowned conferences.

Now, during the holidays, Lise listened to people talking about the latest babies being born and holiday meals being prepared. She felt detached, the same way she had as a young child when she discovered an insatiable love for learning, puzzles, and, science.

Despite her solitude, she knew she was lucky. Lise was Jewish by birth, which made her a target of the Nazi government in Germany. For the past five years, Jewish scientists had been fleeing Germany to escape Nazi persecution. Friends had managed to smuggle Lise out in July, but she had to leave behind almost thirty years of work in Berlin.

As she waited for her nephew to join her, Lise's thoughts turned to Hahn, who was still working at the Kaiser Wilhelm Institute. His latest letter contained startling news of his experiments with Fritz Strassmann. She perused it again. Given Frisch's work in nuclear physics, she knew he would be intrigued.

Otto Hahn had written to Lise Meitner looking for guidance, for an explanation that would put his puzzling results in a physics context. He was depending on her, just as he had always depended on her since they first teamed up in 1907.

By then Hahn had been researching radioactive substances for a year at the University of Berlin's Chemistry
Institute. Before Berlin, he had studied radioactivity at
McGill University in Canada under noted physician Ernest
Rutherford, who had codeveloped the theory that elements
could disintegrate and transform into other elements. But
back in Germany, radium research was so new that the
organic chemists at the institute didn't take his work seriously, and he had nobody to collaborate with. He was
shunted off to the school's old basement workshop to conduct his radiation experiments.

Hahn found the physicists at the university a bit friendlier and regularly attended the Wednesday physics colloquium. It was there that he had met Lise Meitner. She had
recently moved from Vienna to attend the lectures of the
theoretical physicist Dr. Max Planck and was looking to fill
her free time doing experimental work. Knowing her interest
in radioactivity, the director of the university's Physics Institute had suggested she work with Hahn.

Close in age, the two young scientists liked each other
immediately. Hahn's informal demeanor made Lise feel
comfortable asking questions, and Hahn was glad to find
another scientist who shared his interest in radioactivity.
Together, their different physics and chemistry backgrounds
allowed them to conduct and analyze experiments they
couldn't accomplish on their own.

There was just one small glitch: Hahn worked for Emil

Fischer, who ran the Chemistry Institute. Fischer did not like female students and scientists and forbade them from working in his laboratory. Hahn asked Fischer to make an exception for Lise. She would be an excellent addition to the institute, he told Fischer. She had the right background, which would enhance the institute's status; Lise Meitner would be the physicist, while Otto Hahn would be the chemist. Fischer relented, saying that as long as Lise would agree to stay in the old basement workshop with the radiation equipment, she could work with Hahn. She was told that this would be only a temporary situation, but as it turned out, her stay in the basement extended to five years.

On occasion, when no one was looking, Lise would quietly leave her office and walk up the creaking staircase, down the corridor, and into the lecture halls. There she would huddle under the benches and for the next hour or two listen to the presentations. She yearned to sit with the rest of the male scientists, but it seemed like an unsurpassable barrier. When the lectures and presentations were over, she returned to the basement. It upset Lise that such attitudes persisted in a university setting.

Once a month, she made the trek to the post office to collect the money her family sent her, as her position at the university was unpaid. She supplemented her allowance with money from writing and translating scientific articles and lived frugally, often surviving on coffee and dry bread.

Her financial situation changed nominally when in 1912

Dr. Planck made her his assistant, her first paid academic post. The stipend was scant, but it came at the right time, because her father had died and her family was struggling to provide Lise with an allowance. At that same time, the new Kaiser Wilhelm Institute for Chemistry opened in Berlin. Otto Hahn was offered a salaried position in charge of radioactivity; Lise was invited to join him as an unpaid "guest."

In her new lab, no one paid attention to the vapors that wafted from the large bowls of mercury left out in the open, or to the beads that fell from the bowls and became embedded in floorboards and cracks on the table. Mercury's dangers were not known, or perhaps were simply ignored. The scabs that were forming on their fingertips were not thought to be associated with the mercury, and it was only when a member of their team died of carcinoma that the connection was made.

Soon after starting work in the laboratory, Lise began to experience headaches and terrible nausea. Oddly enough, on a visit to Austria to see her family, the symptoms disappeared. She did not connect her pain to the poisonous atmosphere that surrounded her, and credited the cure to the fact that in Austria she felt less stressed.

The environment at the Kaiser Wilhelm Institute suited Lise Meitner, and in 1934 she was eventually hired as an associate. Several years later she became a professor in charge of her own physics department. The study of radioactivity was rapidly leading to exciting discoveries, and the early 1930s proved to be fruitful years in atomic research. A major breakthrough occurred not in some dusty laboratory in Europe, but in the United States. It was in New York, in a laboratory headed by Dr. Harold C. Urey, that a group of physicists discovered deuterium, a stable isotope of hydrogen. Also called "heavy hydrogen," it would have a great impact on atomic research. Then, in 1932, the neutron was discovered in England, followed two years later in France by the Joliot-Curies' discovery of artificial radioactivity. This set Fermi to bombarding elements with neutrons, which led to the experiments in Berlin.

In Italy, Fermi was excited by this new discovery. He was thirty-one years old and had been waiting for something new to occupy his mind. When deuterium was discovered, he decided this would be the element he would "play with" the most. Fermi and his colleagues brought a list to the chemical shop of all the elements they needed to buy in order to bombard them. Fermi and his staff bombarded these elements with neutrons, and this included uranium.

Lise, like other scientists, kept tabs on all this activity. It was how research was conducted, how everyone worked. Everyone followed what everybody else was doing.

As the years passed, new elements were discovered by almost every scientist working in the field. And while in the laboratories across Europe work continued at a feverish pace, social concerns began to trickle in from the outside world.

Adolf Hitler became chancellor of Germany in 1933. Seen at first as a fringe figure of the radical far right, Hitler rose to power trading on people's misery and fear during the worldwide economic depression and desperation of the previous few years. Through relentless propaganda and fiery rhetoric, Hitler and the Nazi Party blamed Jews, Communists, and a weak government for Germany's woes, and hatred and violence toward Jews increased. Lise had picked up Hitler's book, *Mein Kampf,* when it was first published. Not wanting to spend money on it, she thumbed through it while browsing in a bookshop and was shocked by its tone and anti-Jewish message. She quickly put it down, unable to digest its contents. Inside the laboratories, scientists moved on with their work.

By 1938, Lise Meitner and her group had managed to find nearly a dozen radioactive substances within uranium bombarded by neutrons. They were satisfied with their research and their work, and life would have progressed in a similar fashion if Germany had not annexed Austria in March of that year, introducing new regulations under which Jews now had to lead their lives. Although Lise had been living in Berlin for many years, she was an Austrian Jew, and so those new regulations applied to her.

The dark moods that had become widespread outside the laboratory began to worry the scientists, too. Lise read the daily newspapers and kept watch on the activities happening around the city and the country. Everywhere she looked, the news was grim. But Otto Hahn assured her that she had nothing to be concerned about. Why would she fear Adolf Hitler? he asked. She reminded him that aside from being Austrian, she was also Jewish. Although she had never hidden her background, she had not flaunted it, either. It was, her father had taught her, just part of her heritage. He had also taught her to reject the notion that she was inferior because of her Jewish blood. Yet now she was worried because of it—not everyone held the same beliefs that her father did.

Hahn didn't think that Hitler's new regime would last long. It would break apart soon enough, he thought, and no one would ever hear about that little man again. Hahn was so confident about this that Lise's concerns seemed almost childish to him. He was preparing to leave the country for a semester of lectures at Cornell University, in Ithaca, New York, that would keep him in the United States for more than four months, and nothing she said seemed to bother him. He was looking forward to getting away and didn't want anything to stop him. In fact, the possibility of postponing the trip never dawned on him.

But Lise felt afraid, and it seemed to her that after so many years of working together and their long friendship, Hahn was deserting her. She begged him to stay and help her through this difficult moment, to assist her in coming up with a plan of action. But he wouldn't hear of it. Actually, he thought she had become very unreasonable and too emotional. It was unbecoming of her, a side of her personality that he had never seen before and that he didn't appreciate. She was like all the others: too sensitive and dramatic, something he had not expected from her.

Six weeks after Hahn left for the United States, the Kaiser Wilhelm Institute for Chemistry was flying a flag with the swastika, and Lise was left trying to understand what it meant for her scientific community.

Germany's most famous scientist, Albert Einstein, had very publicly resigned from the Prussian Academy of Science and renounced his German citizenship. "I do not intend to put my foot on German soil again as long as conditions in Germany are as they are," he said.

Lise regretted the loss. She had first met Einstein in 1909 at a conference in Salzburg, Austria, where she had also given a report. Einstein had rattled the audience with his startling concept that light must behave like both an undulating wave and a stream of particles. But what Lise most remembered all these years later was how easily and logically he had explained his special theory of relativity, deriving from it the equation $E = mc^2$ and showing "that to every radiation must be attributed an inert mass." As a physicist just starting out, she had found this idea "overwhelmingly new and surprising."

Although the wave-particle theory of light had gone over her head, she had been impressed. Einstein was a few months younger than she and already a star, having published his theory of relativity in 1905 at the age of twenty-six. And he had done it while earning a paycheck as a clerk, plodding away in the Swiss patent office. He, too, had once had trouble finding a paid academic position.

Later, Lise had become acquainted with Einstein on a more personal level in the home of her mentor Dr. Max Planck, and she had often listened to the two physicists play chamber music in the evenings, with Einstein on violin and Dr. Planck on piano.

On April 7, 1933, the news was even worse. The Nazis passed their first race law, barring Jews from all civil service. Suddenly 20 percent of the university scientists in the country were dismissed, including Lise's nephew, Otto Robert Frisch, in Hamburg. Others resigned in protest, most notably Nobel laureate James Franck at the University of Göttingen. Although his status as war veteran allowed him to remain at his post despite his Jewish heritage, he refused to serve a state that treated its Jewish citizens as alien enemies.

The dismissal sent a slew of scientists out of Germany to countries that welcomed them. The emigrants sought the freedom to continue their work in an environment where their skills and knowledge would be seen as an asset, not a threat. They spread out across Europe, with several settling in England. Others ended up in the United States, eventually working on a secret military operation to end the war Hitler would start in 1939. The very people Hitler seemed to want to shun would be just as eager to bring about his end.

To Lise, the departures of Frisch and Franck and so many others was a real blow. For the moment, though, her position seemed safe. The Kaiser Wilhelm Institute, funded partially by industry, had never been under direct government control, and she was an Austrian citizen. But she felt isolated in an institute where colleagues were showing up for work in the brown shirts of the Nazi Party. She spent many sleepless nights worrying about the future but continued working in the lab and filling in for Hahn as institute director.

Lise regularly kept him updated, and by May she was imploring Hahn to return quickly after his semester at Cornell was over and not travel to California, as he was now planning to do.

That month Dr. Planck, as president of the Kaiser Wilhelm Society, visited Hitler to pay his respects to the new chancellor. Unbeknownst to Lise at the time, Dr. Planck took the opportunity to speak up for his Jewish colleagues. By then a world-famous Nobel laureate, he argued that "forcing worthy Jews to emigrate would be equivalent to mutilating ourselves outright, because we direly need their scientific work and their efforts would otherwise go primarily to the benefit of foreign countries." Hitler was not interested in rational discussion, however, and went off on one of his notorious rants, working himself into such a fit that the dignified scientist could only sit quietly until he was permitted to withdraw. The Nazis would harass him for years for his sympathies, but Dr. Planck never spoke of the "horror" of that meeting to his colleagues until after the war.

Hahn returned to Berlin in July. By then the Nazis had set upon a course of systematically pushing "non-Aryans" out of German life. Lise's Austrian citizenship continued to protect her as laws stripped German Jews of their citizenship and all civil rights. Race laws restricted the jobs Jews could hold, the businesses they could own, and even the things they could buy.

But on March 13, 1938, Lise's protection disappeared overnight. Germany annexed Austria, and suddenly the race laws applied to her.

As much as it pained her, Lise realized that she had to leave her beloved laboratory and give up her life in Berlin. It was only a matter of time before she would lose her job. Niels Bohr invited her to Copenhagen, but when she applied for a visa, the Danish consulate would not accept her Austrian passport. She had to seek new documents from the Nazi government. Of course her request was denied. By then the Nazis were restricting Jews' travel abroad. As a scientist, she was expressly forbidden to leave.

Lise's options were limited. Only the Netherlands and Sweden were likely to accept her with an Austrian passport, and a paid position as a physicist was hard to come by since so many scientists had left Germany. Her friends abroad worked tirelessly on her behalf, and Bohr finally found her a position in Stockholm. All she had to do was get out quietly and quickly before the Nazis officially sealed the border against her. She almost decided not to leave, afraid that she'd be arrested, but on July 13, 1938, she boarded a train and, accompanied by a Dutch friend, crossed into the Netherlands without incident. Lise was safe.

In a laboratory in Rome that July, Enrico Fermi was concerned. He was the most prominent physicist in Italy, with his laboratory full of the best minds in the country. He had brought fame and honor to his beloved country with his research on radiation and the effects of slow neutrons. But for the past two years, Italy's fascist government had been Germany's ally, and now it had finally embraced Hitler's racist ideology. Fermi's wife, Laura, was Jewish. If similar race laws were passed, Laura would fall prey to them, and so would their children. It did not matter how famous he was or what he could provide to their country: Italy would have no mercy. He would have to leave as well. He had to come up with a plan.

Lise Meitner had not been happy about the idea of leaving Berlin. At that time, she was not sure she wanted to go to Stockholm. She would have preferred England, where she had friends and the development of atomic physics was already under way. However, thanks to a friend, the offer to work at Manne Siegbahn's new Nobel Institute for Experimental Physics was her only secure option. From the Netherlands, she flew to Copenhagen, where she was met by the friendly and familiar face of her nephew, Otto Robert Frisch. She spent a few days there with Niels Bohr and his wife before heading on to Sweden.

Naively, she had believed things would work out as they had in Berlin. Unfortunately, unlike Hahn, Siegbahn was not happy to have a woman in his institute, and the spirit of collegiality that had permeated the Kaiser Wilhelm Institute in Berlin was nowhere to be found in Sweden.

The new laboratory held no appeal for her. It was sterile, plain and white, and it still lacked all the necessary equipment for conducting experiments. But what she missed most were her companions; she longed for the friendships she had built during the years alongside Hahn and Strassmann and hovered over the experiments that had yielded so much to her.

Then one day she had a visitor—two, actually. A small, slightly balding man, accompanied by an attractive woman, entered her laboratory, shouting her name. Confusion turned to shock when she realized who had come to visit. Fermi and his wife, Laura, were in the country to pick up the Nobel Prize he had been awarded for his work with neutrons. Lise was flattered by the visit. As he introduced the two women to each other, Enrico noticed that Lise looked tired and worried and wore the tense expression that all refugees had in common. Laura also sympathized with Lise's dilemma of being in a country that was not her own.

The Nobel Prize had given Fermi's family the excuse they had been looking for, not only with a financial reward but also the ability to travel. They had been able to go abroad as a family, and now that they were out of Italy, they were not going back. In about ten days, they would be sailing to the friendlier shores of the United States. He hoped one day to meet Lise again under better circumstances.

Unlike the work Lise was now performing in Stockholm on her own, much of the work she had done at the Kaiser Wilhelm Institute in Berlin had been a joint effort between three scientists: herself, Hahn, and Strassmann.

One winter morning when her nephew Otto Robert Frisch joined her for breakfast, she handed him Hahn's latest letter. On December 19, 1938, Hahn wrote, he and Strassmann had bombarded uranium with a radium-beryllium neutron gun. The result was a small sample that performed like barium, something that could not possibly be. Could Lise make any sense of that? Uranium, atomic number 92, could not suddenly change into barium, atomic number 56, could it? It was a loss of thirty-six units on the element scale. Frisch thought it must be a mistake, but Lise assured him that Hahn was too good a chemist for that.

It was a curious letter, providing a puzzle for Lise to solve. And she had always loved a good puzzle. The idea was almost unimaginable. When neutron experimentation had started, everyone found results that did not fit the expected pattern. Fermi in Rome could not come up with a solution that he deemed convincing. Irène Joliot-Curie and Pavle Savić, and even Hahn and she herself had all thought that the nuclei had captured the neutrons and created new elements heavier than uranium. But now, after a second and third look, Hahn and Strassmann had found something lighter. Maybe, Lise thought, it was not that the neutrons were behaving inappropriately; it was that the scientists who were thinking about the issue were doing so with a closed mind. Perhaps a new rule had to be developed, one adapted to this problem that, if one really thought about it, was not really a problem at all but simply a new surprise, something to force scientists to think more critically about an issue.

She could not recall anyone saying that an atom could not be split in two. Going back to the seminar she had attended with Einstein, she remembered his words precisely: "There is not the slightest indication that energy [in the nucleus] will ever be obtainable," he had told his audience. "It would mean that the atom would have to be shattered." But really, what had he said? Lise wondered. It all depended on how one interpreted his statement. It didn't mean that it could not be done. What Einstein had suggested was that to do so, to get to the nucleus, one really had to split it in two portions. And so far, no one had done it.

Lise and Frisch went off for a walk as they tried to sort out the puzzle. Clearly, the lighter barium had to be a fragment of the uranium nucleus, but how had it happened? Neutrons never broke anything other than a proton or alpha particle away from the nucleus, or so they thought. And a nucleus wasn't a brittle solid that could be chipped or cracked or broken. They remembered the physicist George Gamow's theory that a nucleus was more like a liquid drop. What if they could split into smaller drops, gradually stretching, constricting, and finally turning into two drops? It would look something like a dumbbell. The physicists knew that the surface tension of ordinary drops resisted such division, but nuclei were no ordinary drops. They were electrically charged, and that diminished the effects of surface tension.

Lise calculated that the electrical charge of uranium was indeed strong enough to overcome the surface tension, so the nucleus could possibly be unstable enough to divide when a neutron struck it. But the electrical charge of the two new drops would repel, driving them apart at a high speed. Where would that energy come from? Lise remembered Einstein's equation from that conference so many years ago, $E = mc^2$. She worked out the masses of the new nuclei, and Frisch calculated the energy needed for the repulsion. It all fit.

It was the breakthrough that explained everything, and it had come on a snowy day in Sweden.

Frisch returned to Copenhagen and promptly told his boss, Niels Bohr, of their speculation. Bohr agreed with their theory immediately and urged them to publish a paper. Lise and Frisch decided to write a one-page note about their theory, backed up by physical evidence of the nuclear fragments. They consulted repeatedly over the telephone, the line between Copenhagen and Stockholm as crackly as the ice outside.

Frisch designed a physics experiment to detect the fragments by measuring the bursts of ions they produced. It worked perfectly. Proof in hand, he wrapped up the final paper. Now ready to let the world know of this nuclear fission, he sent their note to the British journal *Nature*.

Frisch's note to the journal read in part: "It seems therefore possible that the uranium nucleus has only a small stability of form, and may, after neutron capture, divide itself into two nuclei of roughly equal size (the precise ratio of sizes depending on finer structural features and perhaps partly on chance). These two nuclei will repel each other and should gain a total kinetic energy of c. 200 MeV, (mega-electron volt) as calculated from nuclear radius and charge. This amount of energy may actually be expected to be available from the difference in packing fraction between uranium and the elements in the middle of the periodic system. The whole 'fission' process can thus be described in an essentially classical way."

It was a startling note, one that would have profound repercussions across the world. In time, some would point to this moment in history as the start of the atomic age, and to Lise Meitner as the originator of the atomic bomb.

chapter six

A Secret Project

1938–1939

I t was not surprising that Niels Bohr was the first to learn of nuclear fission from Otto Robert Frisch. By then Bohr was fifty-four years old, a Nobel laureate, and considered the foremost physicist in the world. He was very excited about this discovery by his longtime friend Lise Meitner and her nephew.

In December 1938, during a lecture in Copenhagen, which was later printed in *Niels Bohr's Times: In Physics, Philosophy, and Polity*, he said, "With present technical means it is, however, impossible to purify the rare uranium isotope in sufficient quantity to realize the chain reaction." As it happened, not far from him, in Stockholm, Lise Meitner was also making a discovery that December that would lead to what he had until then believed to be impossible.

Bohr was preparing to attend the fifth Washington Conference on Theoretical Physics, to be held the following month. His mind had been churning since hearing the news and continued to do so throughout the nine-day transatlantic journey to the United States. He arrived in New York on January 16, 1939, nearly two weeks after the Fermis had docked there. In fact, it was Enrico Fermi who met him at the pier.

By the time he took to the conference podium to share his news, Bohr was positively bubbling over with enthusiasm. He had prepared his remarks on a stack of papers that he held in front of him, but then, looking out at his audience, he swept his notes aside and began to speak freely, as if in front of one of his classes. Fission, he told the audience, referred to the moment when the nucleus of an atom split into two fragments.

As Bohr relayed the information to his colleagues, all of them could feel the electricity running through the auditorium. Although some of the information had been leaked prior to Bohr's talk, hearing the news from Bohr's own lips allowed the news to be received with enthusiasm and not even the smallest amount of skepticism. Still, they wanted Bohr to end his speech as soon as possible. It was impolite to get up and leave in the middle of a talk, but they wanted to rush to their own laboratories and check the experiments themselves. Once they did, the theory of nuclear fission would become widely accepted.

A few of these scientists wondered why they had not observed the phenomenon before. Others boasted of having come close to the solution themselves; whether or not that was true, they agreed that they should have stayed with the experiments a little longer.

It was a startling moment, not only for Lise Meitner's breakthrough but also for nuclear science in general. Many of the scientists in attendance, much like Lise Meitner, would come to the realization that nuclear fission could form a self-sustaining chain reaction—which in turn, if properly utilized, could form a bomb.

Enrico Fermi was in attendance at the Washington conference. Colleges and universities across the United States were hiring professors who were fleeing the racial persecution in Europe, and Fermi, having received the Nobel Prize in Physics in 1938, had been quickly offered jobs at five different universities; he accepted a teaching post at Columbia University in New York City. The university felt it was a real coup to land a man like Fermi, and he did not disappoint.

Soon after the conference ended, Fermi urged his supervisors at Columbia University to repeat the tests that had been conducted in Europe. If they were successful, he told them, they should begin to study the possibilities of a long-range chain reaction. The Columbia laboratory was led by Fermi along with Leo Szilard, a Hungarian émigré. Both of them had fled Europe because of the Nazis, and now it was their job to determine whether or not a chain reaction was possible, and how that could be used against the enemies.

Fermi succeeded in performing a small experiment related to nuclear fission by showing that uranium bombarded by neutrons emitted more neutrons than it absorbed. The Columbia group released a statement saying, "This new process gives the largest conversion of mass into energy that has yet been obtained by terrestrial methods." The words were a little outlandish and pompous, given that in Europe Fritz Strassmann and Otto Hahn had been conducting those same experiments for months. But then, Fermi was an extravagant man.

From this point on, scientists pursued studies and experiments on fission with abandon, and hundreds of papers were written and published, outlining the methods for fission without regard for who would be at the receiving end of that knowledge. Countries around the world began thinking that fission might be used for military purposes.

Although Americans' larger aim was to create a nuclear bomb, they had to tackle the questions that came first: They needed to understand how the finer details of nuclear fission worked and whether or not they could control it. Once they got a handle on those things, they could move forward.

Scientists studied these concepts and continued to publish their results. Publication was the natural outcome of years of research, hours of hard and dedicated work, sometimes tedious, at other times exciting. These articles could be read by anyone. Soon, a voluntary ban against publishing research was instituted by the British as well as by those working in the United States. However, the French team, led by the Joliot-Curies, refused to adhere to any ban. They had difficulty accepting the fact that the Nazis might be considering the possibility of constructing a bomb and might be looking to their work for inspiration. And so they continued publishing.

In 1935, Frédéric Joliot-Curie, while delivering a lecture, included the following paragraph: "If, turning towards the past, we cast a glance at the progress achieved by science at an ever-increasing pace, we are entitled to think that scientists, building up or shattering elements at will, will be able to bring about transmutations of an explosive type, true chemical-chain reactions. If such transmutations do succeed in spreading in matter, the enormous liberation of usable energy can be imagined. But unfortunately, if the contagion spreads to all the elements of our planet, the consequences of unleashing such a cataclysm can only be viewed with apprehension."

Not surprisingly, while listening to Niels Bohr at the Washington conference, some in the audience immediately began to speculate about what kind of weaponry such a discovery could offer. For the military, this could be quite a coup. Up until that point, the notion of a bomb based on the principle of a chain reaction was still an abstract concept in the minds of a few who believed it could never come to fruition—at least not during their lifetimes.

But the discovery of nuclear fission discussed at the Washington conference, and the possibility of it being used for weapons, came at the right moment. There were already hints of war, and it was widely believed that Hitler and his regime would be using methods of warfare previously unheard of. One had to fight fire with fire, but there were questions to contend with: If a chain reaction could be achieved, could it also be sustained, or would the reaction speed up and release energy without assistance, basically uncontrolled? Would it shut itself off whenever it wanted to? Could scientists basically control it?

By the summer of 1939, the Americans believed that Germany had already started its own research program, wanting to be the first to develop an atomic weapon, with the British following close behind. Work was also under way in the Soviet Union, where the possibility of an atomic bomb had been discussed and a proposal appeared in 1940. (The Soviet scientific community had discussed the possibility of an atomic bomb throughout the 1930s, going so far as to make a concrete proposal in 1940, but they initiated their program only during World War II, in 1942.)

Although American scientists believed that a fission chain reaction was possible, they were also aware that many obstacles stood in their way. For starters, not every atom could be split in two, though uranium could, especially rare-form uranium-235, which accounted for only 0.72 percent of the naturally occurring element. It was already difficult to separate a large enough amount of identical uranium isotopes for a laboratory reaction; to do it on an industrial scale seemed almost impossible.

Szilard had listened carefully to all that was said at the conference, and he left with two things on his mind: the realization that there was military potential for a nuclear weapon; and the knowledge that the Germans were already very much aware of that potential and were likely working on a bomb.

Szilard realized that the United States and its laboratories had become the beneficiaries of much of the knowledge brought forth by the exiled European scientists. But he was also aware that many other scientists had stayed behind, and they were still working in Germany—for Adolf Hitler. They might have already come up with plans to hand over to Hitler a weapon the likes of which the world had never seen.

Szilard didn't know whether people would listen to him or his ideas. Small in stature and rather round, he liked to sit in a wide chair when deep in thought and cross his hands over his protruding belly. Some thought he had a flair for the dramatic, a reputation he didn't particularly like. But in this case, he was correct in thinking that this was an important matter that needed to be studied with special attention. He was sure that many of the new discoveries had to be kept secret, for fear that they would land in the wrong hands. In fact, he was the one who spearheaded the voluntary publication ban.

Fermi had this to say about Szilard: "He is certainly a very peculiar man, extremely intelligent.... He is extremely brilliant and...he seems to enjoy startling people.... Contrary to perhaps what is the most common belief about secrecy, secrecy was not started by generals, was not started by security officers, but was started by physicists. And the man who is mostly responsible for this certainly extremely novel idea for physicists was Szilard."

It was necessary, he decided, to bring the president into the equation. But Szilard knew where he stood in the great scheme of things. He was not the most famous of the scientists who had come to America. While at times that fact pained him, he realized that this was not the time for petty thoughts. He asked some of his colleagues and friends, including Einstein, to help write a letter to President Roosevelt explaining the possibilities of what they were looking into.

Einstein had become one of the most recognizable scientists, thanks in part to his theory of relativity, which, in truth, few could really understand. Aside from his own celebrity status, Einstein had also elevated the status of physics itself. Americans had immediately fallen in love with this man, who was seen by all as a shy genius, a bit of a scatterbrain who could laugh at himself, and highly unpretentious. They loved those who were associated with him, too, assuming that geniuses ran in packs.

Initially, Einstein had not wanted anything to do with atomic projects. But with the discovery of nuclear fission, he realized that chain reactions could be used with devastating results. Although the general implications of an atomic bomb were already hinted at, Einstein agreed the president must be told of the physicists' concerns.

Einstein warned President Roosevelt that building a superbomb was now very much a possibility. Most scientists feared that the Germans might already be working on such a thing and believed that the United States had to beat them at their game. It would be devastating if the Germans succeeded first.

"Certain aspects of the situation which have arisen," Einstein advised the president, "seem to call for watchfulness and, if necessary, quick action on the part of the Administration."

Einstein urged the president to maintain contact with nuclear physicists through a confidante who could do the following:

a) to approach Government Departments, keep them informed of the further development, and put forward recommendations for Government action, giving particular attention to the problem of securing a supply of uranium ore for the United States;

b) to speed up the experimental work, which is at present being carried on within the limits of the budgets of University laboratories, by providing funds, if such funds be required, through his contacts with private persons who are willing to make contributions for this cause, and perhaps also by obtaining the co-operation of industrial laboratories which have the necessary equipment.

In fall 1939, Alexander Sachs, an economist who worked as President Roosevelt's adviser, brought Einstein's letter to the president. This letter would eventually trigger the Manhattan Project in 1942. Sachs convinced President Roosevelt that the United States, much like other countries, needed to explore the possibility of a fission weapon. President Roosevelt agreed, and the Advisory Committee on Uranium was quickly formed. Money was set aside for buying uranium, and contracts were awarded to various schools across the country, including Columbia, Cornell, and Johns Hopkins, in Baltimore, Maryland, as well as organizations such as the Carnegie Institution for Science, for advanced scientific studies of uranium.

It was from these universities and their laboratories that scientists would eventually be recruited for the Manhattan Project. These men and women, who had been studying nuclear science and anything related to it, were believed to possess the skills and knowledge that the country needed. It was that knowledge that was important, regardless of a scientist's gender. Many employers would not have considered women for work a man could do, but some of the sharpest minds in the new field belonged to women, and they were needed.

And so, instigated by the belief that the Germans were building atomic bombs, many women scientists made their way to the laboratories. Those who joined the project saw this as their patriotic duty; it was their job to help the government, to help stop a madman who could kill millions of people with the push of a button. They were eager to serve in whatever capacity necessary.

Three main sites would eventually be chosen. To provide fuel for the bomb, Oak Ridge, Tennessee, was selected as the site to enrich uranium, and Hanford, Washington, as the site produce the plutonium. At a third site, scientists would design and build the bomb. This spot needed a certain amount of isolation but also easy transportation. There had to be abundant water available, and mountains had to surround the site. It would be only a small facility, officials initially thought: a small laboratory where a few scientists would hash out the final details of the bomb's design. But, as it turned out, Los Alamos, New Mexico, defied everyone's expectations.

Neither Fermi, Szilard, nor any of the Hungarian scientists would take the lead at any of these facilities. Following the attack on Pearl Harbor on December 7, 1941, they were classified as enemy aliens and thus could not be put in charge of such secret affairs, though they still could work on them. And so they continued to study and research at a feverish pace.

Through it all, James Franck, who had joined the Metallurgical Laboratory at the University of Chicago, urged officials to come up with guidelines for the weapons, should they come to fruition. They should be used only under extreme circumstances, Franck said, and only as a last resort. But few gave much thought to what he was proposing. Their focus was on finishing the bomb as soon as possible.

But then something spectacular happened. A new element arrived on the block, an element that could shift things completely and help in the production of the weapon. Scientists learned that uranium-238 could absorb neutrons, thus becoming uranium-239. This, in turn, emitted beta particles, becoming the first human-made element, eventually called neptunium-239. Neptunium-239 also went through a process of exhibiting beta decay, which changed into plutonium-239. And just like uranium, plutonium was found to have the power to fission, or split in two. When bombarded by neutrons, plutonium also released huge amounts of energy. It was a stunning discovery, as scientists now had two paths to building the atomic bomb.

By this point, it was 1941 and Lise Meitner was still in Sweden, away from the Nazis, not knowing that her discovery of fission had laid the groundwork for this secret military operation. The women who would arrived in Oak Ridge, in Hanford, in Los Alamos, and in the various laboratories across the country followed in Lise's footsteps and saw her as their guide, a woman who had helped steer their careers. To them she was a benevolent, brilliant, groundbreaking inspiration, much as Marie Curie had once been to Lise. Once Lise learned of the intentions of the Manhattan Project and found out how her discovery was being used, she would be repulsed. She would not be the only one to feel that way.

TWO

Bomb Making in America

chapter seven

Two of a Kind

1939

n attendance at the start of the Washington conference on January 26, 1939, were the scientists Joseph Mayer and Maria Goeppert-Mayer. They listened attentively to Niels Bohr as he talked about Otto Hahn and Fritz Strassmann's discovery, as well as Lise Meitner's subsequent theory of nuclear fission. When Bohr finished, the Mayers, with their friend Robert Fowler, another scientist, rushed out and hopped into their car.

As soon as they arrived home in Baltimore, they prepared a large pot of coffee, spread sheets of paper on their large oak table, and began to make calculations.

When Maria Goeppert was a child, her father, Friedrich Goeppert, had insisted that she find something purposeful to do, something that she'd love and that would provide an income so that she would not need a man to take care of her. And so she had. Her father's views were progressive at the time, as she would later realize. While most women focused on housekeeping and childbearing, Maria, as her father always said, was too exceptional to fall into that routine. He was a professor of medicine at the University of Göttingen, the sixth generation of professors in the family, and Maria expected to follow suit. He taught pediatrics and was also the founder of a children's clinic in the city. That he was a doctor with high expectations for his only child might have played a part in his thinking. But Maria did in fact show exceptional aptitude for learning early on, and that had boosted his case.

While Dr. Goeppert might have hoped for a son, he nonetheless enjoyed Maria's company and taught her all he knew. She was a blond and blue-eyed girl with an earnest, pale, round face, eager to please her father but also prone to adventures and mischief. She recalled waking up one morning to find that he had prepared a special pair of glasses for her so that they could watch a solar eclipse together. When the moment arrived, he explained everything that was happening, step-by-step—one of the many scientific lessons he gave her and one of the first to awaken her curiosity.

Born in 1906 in Katowice, Upper Silesia, in Poland, Maria had moved with her parents to the university town of Göttingen, Germany, when she was four years old and never left until she met Joseph Mayer. While she had spent a term at Cambridge University, she thought it likely that she would follow in her father's footsteps, becoming a doctor in their hometown and teaching at the local university.

Maria's mother, Maria, née Wolff, did not work outside the home, but she enjoyed the perks of being a professor's wife. The family employed servants to take over the household duties, while she dedicated herself to socializing and having parties, with the Goepperts' house becoming the place to be, especially during the holidays.

It was a happy home, despite the fact that it was a small family. The Goepperts had wanted more children, but Frau Goeppert had suffered a handful of miscarriages and felt very lucky to have given birth to Maria. So Maria was showered with enough attention for herself and several siblings.

Although Göttingen was considered rural, it was still a very active place, and all activities revolved around its great university. It was officially called the Georgia Augusta, but everywhere it was known as Göttingen, whose motto was *Extra Göttingen non est vita*—outside of Göttingen there's no life. To a certain degree, everyone in town embodied that slogan.

To the delight of Frau Goeppert, the young Maria agreed to learn what were considered the more feminine pursuits of life, such as knitting and crocheting, but Maria never enjoyed them. She was her father's daughter, with a penchant for reading and experimenting and following her curiosity, particularly in high school, where mathematics began to intrigue her. She often gathered her friends in their large home, to her mother's satisfaction. However, it was only to study mathematics, which Frau Goeppert did not understand or approve of.

In 1921, Maria entered the Association for Women's Education and Study, a private school in her town to prepare girls for the university entrance exam. Maria and her parents had never discussed whether she would go to university; she soon realized that she was always meant to.

When she was sixteen years old, her school closed, but rather than transferring to a boys' school for another year to finish her education, she decided to take the university entrance exam a year earlier than planned.

When she arrived at the school in Hanover, where the test was administered, she was a little dejected to see only four other female test takers among a sea of older boys. The boys did not seem concerned, laughing confidently and staring at the girls with open contempt as they took their seats in the little room; boys were always more numerous than girls, and when there were girls in attendance, they made sure to try to make the event as uncomfortable as possible, or so Maria later explained in her own texts. The test was a long one; the written portion lasted a whole week, and it covered the basics of German, English, French, physics, mathematics, history, and other subjects. This was followed by a daylong oral exam.

By week's end, all the girls had passed, but surprisingly, only one of the boys had made it through. He would also attend the University of Göttingen, and one of the examiners, who was a teacher there and who would later become Maria's friend, eventually told her that the boy had not done well but had been admitted because he had seemed like an "earnest" young man.

At the university, Maria developed a reputation for being not only the smartest woman on campus but also the prettiest. Blond and slim, she was immediately very popular, especially in the department of mathematics, the subject she had decided to study. This choice had shocked her teachers, for they had imagined that with her facility for languages she would have been a foreign language teacher. But there were others who were happy with her choice.

In a small town that revolved around the university, it was impossible for people not to know one another. Many professors were familiar with Maria's family and she became a sort of surrogate daughter to some. The Goepperts lived next door to Professor David Hilbert, whose former student, the brilliant Max Born, had become the chair of the theoretical physics department at the university. Professor Hilbert suggested that Maria speak to Born, who would eventually become her mentor.

Though possessing an exceptional mind, Born was also a very fragile man. A phenomenal atomic physicist, he had suffered from various ailments from a very young age. To some he gave the impression of being a typically formal and in-charge type of teacher, and a rather stiff one at that. Only those closest to him were aware of the frequent bouts of depression that overtook him and the darkness that he often battled.

James Franck, a friend of Born's, was also a professor at Göttingen University and he, too, became a friend of Maria. The opposite of Born, Franck was gentle instead of tense, a naturally kind man whose studies brought excitement to the university life.

In Germany the 1920s were known as the "golden twenties" of atomic physics. Because of Max Born's and James Franck's presence at Göttingen, other well-known and promising physicists arrived at the university to study the science of the atom. There was a young Enrico Fermi, who traveled from Italy, and later an even younger J. Robert Oppenheimer, hailing from California. The two men never met in Germany, but matters in the early 1940s would bring them together in the United States as part of a secret military operation with which their names would be forever linked.

While in Germany, the scientists worked, researched, and studied, talking excitedly about the new discoveries. In the United States atomic physics was still a faraway subject, considered to be almost science fiction, but in Europe, and particularly in Germany, great advances were being made. And Maria was surrounded by all of it, soaking it all in.

This nascent field had actually inspired Maria even before she arrived at the university. Her neighbor, Professor Hilbert, was in the habit of giving lectures on the subject at least once a week. He liked to update not only the experts but also the curious on the latest developments, and he often invited his young neighbor to attend, to hear about the sciences and to be introduced to university life and those who were involved in it.

Maria chose to study mathematics mostly because newspapers all over the country were touting the great demand in Germany for female mathematics teachers. There were many jobs to be had in the field, the papers said, and Maria wanted to work after graduation. But after enrolling, she found that physics was becoming more interesting to her.

"Mathematics began to seem too much like puzzle solving," Maria said. "Physics is puzzle solving, too, but of puzzles created by nature, not by the mind of man." She switched courses in 1927, a year that was pivotal in her life not only because of her academic change but also because her father died. The shock of it nearly broke her.

During this time, she turned to Professor Born for support. He became a sympathetic ear, listening to her desperate woes when the moment called for it. Perhaps it was because his own depressive moods made him particularly sensitive to others. Whatever the reason, she found an affinity with him, and she sought his open door whenever she was in need of soothing words.

Across the Atlantic, as Maria Goeppert grieved for her father and dug deeper into the study of physics, Joseph Mayer was wrapping up his doctoral studies in physical chemistry at the University of California, Berkeley, and embarking on post-graduate work. In 1929, he was awarded a generous grant from the Rockefeller Foundation that would allow him to travel to and study at the University of Göttingen.

Having packed his books and said good-bye to his mother and his friends, Joseph Mayer arrived in Göttingen. With the money in his pocket, he immediately bought himself a car. This was followed by whiskey and gin. Then he worried about a place to live. That winter was one of the coldest Europe had experienced in decades, and he realized that he needed to find suitable accommodations very quickly.

Joseph Mayer was born to an Austrian engineer father and an American mother who had worked as a schoolteacher up until Joseph's birth. His mother was energetic and fun, with a great sense of humor—traits that she passed on to her son. Joseph's father, who had died five years before he came to Göttingen, had been the opposite of his wife: a very quiet and reserved man who liked to study. He had graduated from the Sorbonne in France with a degree in applied mathematics and designed bridges for a living. The family had lived in Montreal, Canada, for a while, but after his father retired, they moved to Hollywood, California.

While Mayer was working in Utah for the summer, his friend decided to attend Caltech, and he followed him, entering in 1921 and graduating in 1924, at age twenty. Known as an outstanding student, Mayer applied to graduate school at UC Berkeley, where he got the opportunity to study under Gilbert Newton Lewis, known as the father of physical chemistry.

When Mayer arrived in Germany, he was set to work with Max Born and James Franck, and likely would have met Maria at some point, but their first encounter happened outside the university halls.

By then, Maria had pretty much barricaded herself in the basement of the university with other students, experimenting and learning. Her life revolved around schoolwork and her town, and she was mostly unaware of what was happening beyond the confines of her city. She was deeply involved in her PhD dissertation, and her work took up the better part of her day.

When her father died, her mother started taking in boarders. Their house was large, and she missed the comings and goings of people, the voices that had filled the rooms. The boarders were mostly Frau Goeppert's business; Maria never had anything to do with them. However, the winter of 1929 weighed heavily on Frau Goeppert's health, and she was often ill. As a result, Maria was required to help her with these transactions.

The day Joseph Mayer showed up to ask about the possibility of renting a room, Frau Goeppert was sick again. It was Maria who opened the door. Shy and quiet, she found herself facing a very tall, friendly American who tried his best with the German language. She replied in perfect English.

Joseph was immediately taken with the petite blonde whose blue eyes looked up at him with suspicion, but for her part, she always maintained that she never paid much attention to him until she saw him swimming at the local pool.

As spring arrived, the two began spending a lot of time together, hiking the nearby lands and lounging in the countryside, dancing, and swimming. He had already fallen in love with this young woman who was not only shy and intelligent but also a challenge. It seemed to Joseph that Maria had no intention of going anywhere, and would be hard to remove from her mother's clutches. When she married him, he knew it would be difficult to move her to America.

They were married at city hall, on a mid-January morning, nearly a year after he'd arrived in Germany, then afterward had a party at her mother's house late in the afternoon. Joseph's mother, Kate Mayer, who had already been traveling through Europe, attended the wedding but remained quiet even during the festivities; she seemed stunned by the whole ordeal. The newlyweds spent a week honeymooning in

Berlin, attending the theater and visiting relatives. Then they returned to Göttingen, where Maria finished up her thesis and prepared to take her oral examinations. That she passed was not a surprise, nor was the fact that her mother planned a party to celebrate with family and friends.

Joseph and Maria decided to leave Germany on March 20, along with Joseph's mother. While Joseph was very excited to return to America, Maria was apprehensive, knowing that her mother would be fearful for her own future and for Maria's new life in America. Still, she had to go and leave Germany for what she believed were friendlier shores.

chapter eight

The General and the Scientist

1942

I n the spring of 1942, President Roosevelt instructed the Army Corps of Engineers to begin constructing the factories to manufacture the materials for atomic bombs. The Army Corps of Engineers, a United States federal agency working under the Department of Defense, formed what they called the Manhattan Engineer District, which later became known simply as the Manhattan Project, because the district's first offices were in Manhattan. The Manhattan Project, in essence, was charged with building the bomb from the ground up, and included some sites where the bomb would be designed and put together.

On December 28, 1942, President Roosevelt also authorized $500 million for the Manhattan Project—not realizing that this amount would not be enough. From the time it was established to the end of 1946, the project's cost would jump to $2.2 billion.

When the official job assignment arrived, General Leslie Groves was not very surprised. He had recently overseen the construction of the Pentagon, and while many had disagreed with the militaristic way he had run that project, he had managed to finish it well before the deadline and to save the government a great deal of money. He would have preferred a new assignment abroad, but as an engineer by training, he understood why officials would consider him the best man to take control of the Manhattan Engineer District. It made him feel good to know that he was so highly thought of as to be given the leadership of such a secret project. And he came to believe that if he couldn't do it, neither could anyone else.

General Groves had been sitting in his study in the fall of 1942, looking out at a gorgeous afternoon, when the letter arrived. He was forty-six years old, but his years in the military had given him a weathered, tough exterior that made him appear much older. Most people did not like him, and he knew that. In fact, a handful of them had told him upfront that they found him to be a jerk. He often smiled when remembering those confrontations. He didn't mind being thought of as arrogant and tough. He had learned early on that when workers respected a leader, they performed their jobs a lot more diligently. He believed that a kinder, friendlier demeanor always brought out the worst in employees, who took advantage of those qualities. And he was not that kind of man.

He returned to his desk and looked over what the military had sent him: plans of what they wanted him to do. They were trying to build an atomic weapon, and the largest and most secret facilities in the country were needed. He was just the man to handle such a delicate situation. His task was relatively straightforward, if one stopped to think about it: He had to translate all that the government and the scientists needed to do into reality, to make sure that everything was on hand for their vision to come to life. What was so hard about that?

Glancing over the paperwork again, he realized that even though he was capable of handling the logistical side of the operation, the scientific portion of the plan was clearly out of his league. He did not like dealing with scientists, even if, in his own way, he respected what they were trying to do. He often complained that scientists were unpredictable, that they did not like to take orders, that they did not do what they were told. For their part, they complained that having the colonel hovering over them was not conducive to their work, which was more organic than his strict schedules allowed. He was controlling, they argued.

He recalled having crossed paths with an ambitious, brilliant, and cocky physicist by the name of Dr. J. Robert Oppenheimer, whose ferocious intellect had frightened him almost as much as the dreadful hats he paraded around in.

But while he thought J. Robert Oppenheimer's sense of style was terrible, he knew that he was the perfect person to lead the scientific laboratories.

Oppenheimer was a tall, pale man who had struck Colonel Groves as being lonely. As a young man, Oppenheimer had suffered from tuberculosis, an infectious disease attacking the lungs, at which point his parents had bought a ranch in the mountains of New Mexico as a place for him to recuperate. There, he had whiled away the hours studying Sanskrit. He was brilliant; he knew it, and other people knew it as well. The standards he set for himself were so high that he could never measure up to them, which was why he published his work so rarely; he had deemed only a few of his articles good enough for others to read.

As soon as General Groves offered him the job, Oppenheimer set about bringing together a large group of young theoretical physicists whom he had either already worked with or met before, most of them hailing from Berkeley. Those who weren't already devoted to him soon would become loyal friends, moved by his intelligence, his way of speaking, and his incredible store of knowledge. General Groves was caught up in Oppenheimer's allure.

General Groves had already decided that the project required several large laboratories. Two ways had been found to fuel an atomic bomb: They could separate the chemically identical isotopes of uranium or produce enough plutonium to create the sustained chain reaction.

Up until this moment, most experiments had been conducted in university labs scattered across the country. But General Groves didn't think that was very efficient. If the country was intent on building a superbomb, they needed to have only a handful of working sites, with more experts located within each one of them.

He marked several sites on a map with large Xs and folded the paper, ready for his meetings. He felt pleased that all was working according to his plans.

chapter nine

American Life

hile Maria Goeppert-Mayer did not like the idea of leaving her mother alone, she knew that her own professional life lay outside Germany. There were few female professors in Germany, and when positions became available, the competition was extremely stiff. Maybe in America it would be easier to achieve her goals.

Following their wedding, Joseph and Maria Mayer headed to Baltimore, where Joseph Mayer was going to become an associate professor in chemistry at Johns Hopkins University. During their transatlantic crossing on the SS *Europa*, he told her all he could about America, about the long roads crisscrossing the country, the beach he had enjoyed going to in the summers, trout fishing, Hollywood, and about Baltimore, but as much as Maria tried to picture Maryland, she couldn't. She enjoyed the journey, though she already missed her mother, and an unsettling fear of the United States had quietly overtaken her. That fear was still churning within her stomach when they arrived in New York Harbor on April 1, April Fool's Day, and she wondered whether that was a bad omen. She tried to get the idea out of her mind, but it followed her when they boarded the train to Baltimore.

Everything was new: her home, her country, her husband. She felt disoriented. She wrote long letters to her mother every day; however, Frau Goeppert tried give the newlyweds their space by replying only every now and again. But when her mother hadn't responded in more than one week, Maria paid a tidy sum to phone her, wanting to know why she was not writing. Panicky and jittery, Maria took a while to settle her nerves.

Although Maria had hoped to work at Johns Hopkins alongside her husband—she set her mind on a teaching job or even a research position—the university gave her a tepid reception and didn't offer her an official position. A German professor was employed in the physics department, and he needed an assistant to help with his correspondence and office tasks; she could make a few dollars helping him with those.

She was granted the use of a tiny room—a closet,

really—in the science department, where she could work on her own experiments, and this, she knew, had happened only because her husband worked at the university. The lack of space would have been a problem for most other scientists, but she accepted the small room and made the best of it.

For the moment, she explained in a letter to her mother, they were living in a boardinghouse. They would remain there for a few months to save some money before heading to Ann Arbor, Michigan, for the summer to attend the Summer Symposium in Theoretical Physics. They were going to settle down on their return. Overall, Maria told her mother, she found the United States a difficult country in many respects, and the Americans themselves a rather dull lot. Germany was far more exciting.

She was also surprised to learn that at Johns Hopkins none of the scientists were engaged in quantum mechanics, a subject that was far advanced in Germany. Maria knew that she would have been able not only to teach the subject at the university level but also to instruct some of the university's teachers. To keep her mind nimble on the subject, she and her new husband engaged in some experiments at night, though she missed the opportunity to perform them with her fellow scientists.

After she married Joseph, a side of his personality that she had known about all along became more pronounced: Her husband liked to argue. He particularly liked squabbling about science, abstract ideas, and subjects he thought he could teach her but in which she was already well versed. Maria had no particular liking for animated arguments. She could engage in heated discussions as much as anyone else, but unlike her husband, she didn't lose her temper. He often managed to make her cry, at which point she would run out of the room and wouldn't talk to him for hours. Their lives together took some getting used to.

They arrived in Ann Arbor, Michigan, to learn that Enrico Fermi was to lecture on the quantum theory of radiation. And it was on that first day that Maria met Laura Fermi. The Fermis were still living in Italy, and this was their first visit to America. It gave them a preview of what life would be like down the road, after the Fermis made to move permanently to the United States.

Maria and Laura hit it off right away, and Maria felt that she had found in Laura someone she could become friends with. Maria watched the Italian couple with interest and realized that, much as in her own relationship, Enrico Fermi liked to have the upper hand, while Laura appeared to be very much underinvolved, unlike Maria, who had no intention of allowing Joseph to get away with anything. Joseph, who liked the Fermis, described Enrico as "a very young and pleasant little Italian, with unending good humor, and a brilliant and clear method of presenting what he has to present in terrible English."

Following the summer lectures and classes, Joseph and Maria returned to Baltimore, where they rented a tiny house and Maria became intent on learning to cook.

Before she arrived in America, her mentor, Max Born, had written to his friend in Baltimore, Karl Herzfeld, that Maria would be there soon. Would he be so kind as to look after her? A stiff, shy German, Herzfeld was more than happy to do that. He was also thrilled to teach Maria all he knew about physical chemistry so that they could collaborate on projects together.

Maria was happy when Frau Goeppert arrived in the United States to spend some time with them. Maria's mother remained in Baltimore for five months, living in their small but well-decorated house. But before Frau Goeppert left, Maria was already making plans to return to Germany, because Born had offered her a job that would last throughout the summer of 1931. Her husband would not be joining her.

As with anyone who leaves their home for a new place, Maria, upon her return to Germany, began to make comparisons between Göttingen and Baltimore. Everything seemed much newer and shinier, although chaotic, in the United States. She thought everything looked ancient and old-fashioned in Göttingen, from the kitchens to the bathrooms.

Politically, while the winds of change had already started to blow, she made an effort to look the other way and to convince herself that nothing horrible was on the horizon.

She had not applied to become an American citizen yet, but with the birth of her first child fast approaching, she realized that she wanted her baby to have parents who were American citizens. She worked tirelessly and earned her citizenship in time for the birth. Marianne was born in spring 1933, and while Maria was reveling in Marianne's giggles and tiny movements, at the same time in Germany the Nazis were enacting the first social laws intended to "clean the civil service." Nearly two hundred college professors lost their jobs, including Maria's mentor, Max Born, who left his position at Göttingen voluntarily in support of his colleagues.

For nearly a year after the birth of her daughter, Maria remained a busy stay-at-home mom, enjoying motherhood and doing very little work in her lab at the university. Motherhood was new and special, and she wanted to cherish it.

Besides, she often told Joseph—and herself—she was aware that hardly anyone missed her at Johns Hopkins. She also thought that no one appreciated her contributions and that they tolerated her only because of Joseph's role on the faculty. She was very good in her field and felt secure in that knowledge. But she was never given a voice in university matters; in the department, she was barely more than a volunteer, paid only a few dollars.

Prior to the birth of her child, she had once made the effort to become a more prominent presence when, noticing an empty office on the physics floor, she had asked the administration if she could have it for herself. While she appreciated the space she had been allotted, it was too small for her needs, she told the officials in the department, as her books and equipment were now overtaking the space. But they had refused her, telling her that the lab she already occupied would have to do. When she asked them how much longer she would have to stay in the small room, they had simply shrugged her off. Deep down, she had not been surprised by their response. She was one of many individuals at the university who were accepted only because of their spouses' positions. She knew she could have done so much more. She could have experimented extensively, as she had in Germany, and given more than any of the men, including her husband, if she'd had the opportunity.

Joseph, for his part, liked the idea of his wife working. It was not because of the money, although that helped. He loved science and knew that he could not live without it, nor could she. He knew that Maria loved the challenge science offered and that she could not do without that mental stimulation, either, as much as she enjoyed her time with their daughter. He encouraged her to return to work, even if only part-time. Maria would have done so anyway without his encouragement, although she was grateful that he understood.

In 1937, just as Maria returned to work at the university in her old position, she received a distressing telegram from Germany, informing her that her mother was dying. She sailed to Germany on the SS *Bremen* and arrived home just in time to see Frau Goeppert before she passed away.

Less than a year later, in 1938, Joseph and Maria Mayer's son, Peter, was born. She did not enjoy this pregnancy as much as her first, feeling larger and clumsier than ever before. To keep her mind occupied, the idea occurred to her and Joseph to write a textbook. They set to work each evening on an old Corona typewriter, with Maria doing most of the writing. It was supposed to be a quick and easy book, an exercise to keep her mind off her daily grind, but *Statistical Mechanics* took nearly three years to complete. And it was while working on the book that Joseph Mayer learned that he was being fired from Johns Hopkins.

But he didn't have to worry, as almost immediately Joseph received two job offers with nearly identical pay: one from Columbia University and one from the University of Chicago. He accepted the Columbia position, but despite their good fortune, Maria could not shake the feeling that she had been in some way the cause of his firing.

It did not help matters that her mentor at the university, Professor Herzfeld, and a handful of her other colleagues saw it similarly. They all agreed that, indirectly, her presence at Johns Hopkins had never been a very good thing for her husband. "There was an antifeminine bias among some faculty in the department," Herzfeld told her later. "And perhaps the feeling that three Germans—Maria, Franck, and I—were too many."

But Joseph Mayer didn't care. He had a new job, a good one at that, and *Statistical Mechanics* was finished.

When Joseph and Maria moved to New York, they lived across the Hudson River, in Leonia, New Jersey. There they found the Fermis, who had arrived from Italy in January 1939. Leonia, it appeared, was becoming ground zero for physicists, and for that Maria was grateful. Besides, she liked Laura Fermi and enjoyed her friendship, and the Fermis were parents to two young children, just like Joseph and Maria Mayer. They also shared a disdain for the fascist governments in Europe. Their fear and disgust bonded them.

Statistical Mechanics by Mayer and Mayer was ready to be published. But there was a problem. Joseph's name was to appear on the book as "Joseph Edward Mayer, Associate Professor of Chemistry, Columbia University." But what about Maria? Maria Goeppert-Mayer, what? She was not working for Columbia University, like her husband. Harold Urey, who ran the chemistry department at Columbia, asked his dean if some sort of job could be found for her, if only for the book's sake. But his dean balked at the idea of employing her, either to make use of her expertise or to give her the credentials to use next to her byline.

Seeing that his dean would not hire Maria for full-time work, Urey went ahead and hired her himself half-time to lecture to chemistry students. In the end, "Maria Goeppert Mayer, Lecturer in Chemistry, Columbia University," appeared on the title page. The book, first published in 1940, became an instant classic, solidifying Joseph's reputation. However, its publication didn't do anything for Maria. Much as had happened with Marie Curie when she won the Nobel Prize with Pierre Curie, most people, including the officials at Columbia University, mistakenly assumed that Joseph had been entirely or mostly responsible for the book, from its conception to its execution, and that Maria had only assisted on it. It was Joseph's devotion to his wife that made him want to have her name on the manuscript, the mistaken impression went; it was simply a nod of his love toward her and nothing more.

Following publication of the book, Maria received a job offer from Sarah Lawrence College, in Bronxville, New York; the school wanted to hire her to teach several science and math courses. She didn't have much of an opportunity to prepare, but she decided to take the job anyway. And within days, she found herself teaching chemistry to a group of young women who had much difficulty following her presentations.

While she enjoyed her position at Sarah Lawrence, an

offer that came later in the spring was far more appealing. Harold C. Urey, who had helped her with her Columbia University credentials, invited her to join a secret project at Columbia, where scientists were working feverishly to separate the isotope uranium-235 from the more widely available uranium-238. Maria had already heard rumors about some sort of massive project the country was involved in, but, being so caught up in her work, she had not been able to confirm those reports. Soon those rumors became confirmed when officials came calling on her. The secret research group, she learned, was called the SAM—for Substitute Alloy Materials—Laboratory, of which Urey had become the director. She readily accepted his offer, liking the idea of being hired on her own merits rather than because she was associated with her husband.

Maria quickly learned that the government was busy working on building an atomic bomb to stop Adolf Hitler. She thought of her beloved Germany and of those who lived there, including her family. What would happen to them if such a bomb were dropped on the country?

As she became more knowledgeable about the project, Maria was aware that the scientists were encountering several challenges while working with uranium, including issues with uranium hexafluoride, which was not only poisonous but also highly corrosive. Scientists had to find some kind of roadblock that would go around pipes, pumps, and anything else surrounding the bomb to keep it sealed. Most scientists were naturally skittish about working with hexafluoride, but Maria was not. She was, by nature, fearless, and Urey knew that.

Initially, she had agreed to work on the project half-time, with weekends to herself so that she could spend some time with her children. She wanted to keep up the routines of an everyday life, while in reality she was involved in a highly classified operation, the magnitude of which she could not even begin to imagine.

As the job went on, she was needed more and more, and balancing home life and work life became more troublesome. She left for work early, often before the children woke up, and arrived home late in the evening. And it was not uncommon for her weekends to be taken over by work duties, too. She missed her children and knew that they waited for her in the evening to play, to share homework, to talk about school projects. But she was too tired to do anything but rest on the sofa. A job that was supposed to be part-time had gradually taken over her existence, though she was happy her contribution was proving valuable.

She was torn about what to tell her young children, if anything, about the work she was performing. How would she be able to explain that it was Hitler that they were fighting, not the Germans themselves, and that the United States had nothing against the German people? That said, how would she be able to explain the thousands of people who would die when the bomb dropped? And how would she be able to explain to her daughter, who was old enough to understand, the role she had played in it? Most of all, how would she be able to live with it herself?

chapter ten

Recruiting

J oan Hinton, a graduate student in the physics department at the University of Wisconsin, entered the laboratory to meet her study group and again noticed that something was out of sorts: Another classmate of hers was missing. Lately Joan Hinton had noted that a handful of her fellow students and several of her professors had disappeared. One day they were around—roaming the halls of the university, reading and correcting their papers, holding their cups of coffee—and the next day they were gone. She had mentioned this strange occurrence to other students, as well as to administrators, asking a litany of questions that began in the morning and ended at night, but all of them, students and faculty alike, had shrugged her off. No explanation was ever given for the disappearances. New teachers replaced the missing professors, but the missing students were never spoken of or seen again.

She suspected something shady was afoot and continued to badger those in charge of the department, but no one would answer her, and her concern continued to grow. Then one day she received a letter; someone quietly slid it under the door while she was studying in her room, sitting on her bed, and by the time she hopped off the bed and reached the door, the person who had delivered the letter was gone, the corridor empty.

The letter was as plain as could be, if not for the word CONFIDENTIAL stamped next to her name. She unsealed it and quickly read the few lines describing some war project taking place in a remote location in New Mexico. Would she be interested in joining? the letter asked. She left her room and looked down the corridor again, the letter flapping in her hand.

It was dark; no one was in the corridor. She closed the door and read the words again. The project sounded fascinating, even though the letter didn't go into details. Full of the spirit of adventure and optimism that marked her personality, she mentally accepted and right away headed to the library to find a book related to the location in New Mexico where the letter told her she could soon be heading: Los Alamos.

Having decided to accept the job, Joan realized that there were a few official matters that she needed to deal with. The end of the semester was still some weeks away, but she had to take her final exams before leaving if she hoped to end the school year with good marks.

She was tall, blond, and good-looking—an exuberant young woman known for her eccentricities; there was something about her that surprised people when they learned that she was interested in atomic physics. But it should not have been that astounding. She was smart and witty, and she came from a smart family. Her uncle, G. I. Taylor, was an English physicist and mathematician; and her great-grandfather George Boole was a famous nineteenth-century logician, philosopher, and mathematician who had created Boolean algebra, the basis for computer circuits. She had inherited her smarts.

The day after she received the letter from the Manhattan Project officials, she approached her mathematics professor, Stanislaw Ulam (who would go on to work for the Manhattan Project himself), and asked to take the final examination in classical mechanics a few weeks earlier than scheduled. She told him that she had been hired for some work and that she had been asked to start right away. Professor Ulam didn't press for more details, nor was he surprised by the request. A handful of other students had made such appeals in the past months.

Joan explained that she had already spoken with the chairman of the department, Professor Ingraham, who had given his permission. Thus, Professor Ulam agreed. He quickly wrote out a list of questions on the back of an envelope and handed it to Joan. She sat on the floor of the office in North Hall, ripped out several sheets of paper from a notepad, and scratched out the answers. She handed them to Professor Ulam and left the office. Then, much like many of her fellow students and professors, Joan left the University of Wisconsin, never to be seen on its grounds again.

chapter eleven

Leona

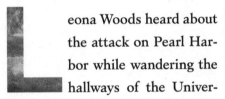

L eona Woods heard about the attack on Pearl Harbor while wandering the hallways of the University of Chicago, where she was a student. It was early December, and the students and faculty were hurrying to finish up the semester in order to get home to their loved ones and indulge in some much-needed rest. But the sudden bombing in Hawaii put everyone on edge.

Leona was working on her PhD thesis in physics and she loved the program. In 1939, she had attended a seminar held by the Nobel laureate James Franck in which he had spoken on Brillouin zones, and this had inspired her to pursue further studies in physics. At the time of her studies, the chairman of the physics department at the university was Arthur Compton. The Advisory Committee on Uranium had assigned Compton the task of building the chain reaction that would be a part of the graphite-uranium pile project, and he was hard at work on the plan. He was supervising the experimental and theoretical studies looking at how to create the first chain reaction, which would eventually give way to an actual explosion. At the time of the Pearl Harbor attack, few were aware of Compton's work. Leona and most of the other students knew him only as the chairperson of their department. While Leona liked Compton, her own professor and thesis chair was another future Nobel Prize winner, Dr. Robert Mulliken.

Leona had started her graduate studies in 1940, working alongside other graduate students who were part of Dr. Mulliken's group, quietly secluded in the basement of the university. Many members of this advanced class now found themselves being called away to do research for Harold Urey at Columbia University in New York. They had not been told what the research entailed, but they had rushed over to Columbia. Leona had not been asked to join that program, something she resented.

Nonetheless, she was glad to be a part of Dr. Mulliken's group, although she felt that she was sort of an anomaly there. In early 1936, Dr. Mulliken had stated in an interview that in his opinion, women didn't show any aptitude for physics, the "father" of all sciences. He had to have realized that there were brilliant women physicists, some of whom had pioneered nuclear research in Europe, research that was the foundation for the work that he himself was now doing and enjoying in Chicago.

However, Dr. Mulliken claimed that there were no women in the United States who could make him change his mind. He hoped that in time he could revise his opinion and see women's contributions in a better light. But for the moment, he believed women were better off teaching in a classroom than experimenting in a laboratory. Eventually he started reading about the up-and-coming female scientists working in American laboratories and universities, as well as teaching some of those female scientists himself, and his thinking began to evolve.

In 1939, Leona and the rest of the group had attended several seminars held by the university on nuclear fission and a range of similar topics, including methods of separating isotopes. She believed the school would continue to organize such lectures, but as the months wore on, these subjects became classified, and scientists were urged not to publish information or even talk about these matters as part of a lecture series. The information given to the students became scantier and scantier. The students noticed this development, talked about it, and wondered why it was occurring.

Aside from being the director of the Chicago lab, Arthur Compton was also a dean in the physics department, and one of the perks of the job was the freedom to get office space and materials for his students, especially laboratory space for those who worked for him, and thus he was very well liked. The physics department shared Eckhart Hall with the math department, but it soon outgrew its space, and Compton pushed the math department to move out, whereupon he barricaded the hall and had it guarded; its doors were eventually sealed, and an armed guard was even posted outside.

Leona observed everything occurring around her with interest. For the third time, she was rewriting her thesis, which Dr. Mulliken was supervising, and while she tried to concentrate on her work, the construction occurring around her also caught her attention. Everything intrigued her, and the secrecy made her wonder.

Compton was considered an extremely good-looking man, who worked hard to keep himself in shape by playing many rounds of tennis and walking several times a day. He was gracious and had the capacity to overlook defects in people. He often invited coworkers and students to his home, and several of the students ended up renting the third floor of the large house where he lived with his wife, Betty. One of the renters included the physicist John Marshall.

Leona had noticed John Marshall at the start of the semester, while deeply involved in her molecular spectroscopy work. John was a scientist, Leona Woods knew, with an intriguing mix of intelligence, interesting looks, and geekiness. Maybe it was because most people described her—a tall young woman with pale skin and an odd hairdo—in similar terms that she felt a connection to him. She learned through some intense inquiries that John was a staff member in Enrico Fermi's laboratory.

These scientists had joined the Substitute Alloy Materials Laboratory when it was originally established at Columbia University; when the Metallurgical Laboratory was established at the University of Chicago, the scientists had moved to Chicago. Leona knew that Leo Szilard, Walter Zinn, Herbert Anderson, and Edward Teller were also involved. The laboratory was so new that she watched as more equipment arrived daily. Because the staff didn't have enough supplies, most of them resorted to helping themselves to whatever materials—glue, pliers, and tweezers—they needed from other departments, promising to return them but never doing so. Leona eventually became the leader of this band of nerdy thieves, her wide pockets always full of office supplies that her coworkers had asked her to retrieve.

Leona had made up her mind to meet John Marshall. So one afternoon, as she was crossing the hallway on her way to the lab, she cornered him while he was smelting metal bricks. John was not a very tall man, but Leona thought him a very handsome one. He came from a large and prosperous family, his father being John Marshall Sr., the director of the DuPont Fabrics and Finishes Department. Szilard had recruited John to Columbia University, but when operations moved to the University of Chicago, so had John. He had already finished his doctoral work and looked forward to the challenges that lay ahead.

Flashing a crooked but confident smile, Leona told him that she knew about the government project he and his team were working on and that she had also heard through the university grapevine that they had discovered how chain reaction worked. And it was true; the sharing of information between students had allowed Leona to keep herself up to date, and whatever she had not been able to learn with certainty, she was capable of figuring out. She clearly suspected what her former classmates and colleagues who had been called to New York had been working on, and she was almost sure of what was being tested at the university. Her certainty showed while she talked with John.

John Marshall was immediately startled, not only because his group had tried to keep their work secret, but also because this young woman, who was obviously very familiar with the sciences and with him, seemed so brash, so much bolder than most women he knew. He was not alone in that opinion. Leona had a reputation for being brazen and blunt; for speaking up when the mood struck her, without a filter between her brain and her tongue; for spewing out ideas that were unpopular, whether scientific ones or personal ones. Not everybody liked her, and she did not mind that. John simply stared at her, eventually leaving her standing in the hallway without saying much of anything. This would become a recurring problem in their relationship, one Leona would not be able to tolerate.

The following day, while changing classes, Leona was approached by Enrico Fermi. She had heard about the Italian Nobel laureate, of course, but had never spoken to him. She was surprised by how short he was; in fact, he stood only about five feet six inches tall, and Leona was much taller than him, nearly six feet tall herself. By then, Fermi had lost most of his dark hair, but he still retained his powerful body, and his blue eyes—which his wife often said were set too close together—were as playful as ever. His shoulders were rounded, with a slight stoop, probably from spending so many hours poring over theoretical problems, and his skin was a pale olive color. Those who didn't know him would have mistaken him for just another random professor crossing the hallways.

In a few simple words, and without any pleasantries, Fermi told Leona that he wanted her to join his staff. He didn't know yet in what capacity she would be used, but he was sure they would find something productive for her to do. She seemed too clever for him not to hire her, he said. And that John Marshall had recommended her to him.

After she nodded in agreement, Fermi asked her what

she thought this project they were working on was about, what she suspected they were building behind those doors that they kept locked and guarded. And without hesitation, Leona told him that she believed they were working on constructing a bomb.

Fermi took off his glasses and wiped them on the sleeve of his shirt. She would learn that he purchased inexpensive pairs of glasses, with various degrees of magnification, at the local drugstore, as he had a tendency to lose his glasses. Indeed, he thought, she seemed too clever for her own good.

Pleased with herself, she said that she would be happy to come on board, appearing as if the idea had never crossed her mind before. But the truth was that she had thought of such a possibility some time before and had planned accordingly by making sure she met the scientists in the corridor.

An astute woman, Leona had understood early on what the government was working on: a bomb to end the war, likely to be used against the Germans. And immediately she wanted to be a part of that plan. She knew that anyone who was anyone in the field was gradually collecting at the University of Chicago. And now she would become part of that exclusive group. She could not imagine what role she would play in the building of the atomic bomb. However, she knew that she would have her hand in history. She joined that illustrious circle in August 1942, never looking back and never asking herself too many questions.

chapter twelve

Coworkers

ermi told his group that Leona would now be a part of their team. He had given it much thought, and had decided that he was so impressed with her work and attitude that she would be assigned several jobs, some more complex than others. For one, she would be taking notes on his lectures, which in turn would be passed on to the crew in charge of building the first pile. An additional task was going to be more complicated: Fermi wanted her to build boron trifluoride counters, which would be used to detect neutron flux in the chain reaction that would eventually be tested.

Nathalie Goldowski was delighted to meet Leona when she joined the laboratory. Although she wouldn't have minded being the only female scientist in the group, having Leona there, she believed, would be a welcome reprieve from the mostly masculine environments she had worked in.

Or so she had expected. But Leona's high-pitched enthusiasm soon wore her out. She was too young, Nathalie thought upon meeting Leona—nearly ten years Nathalie's junior. She was too excitable, too eager to prove herself. Leona needed to tone down her attitude and to refrain from sharing her ideas about the bomb's purpose, about where and when it should be used. One needed to be impartial, Nathalie always told herself. With such a project, personal feelings should be kept in check. Objectivity was required.

But maybe it was Nathalie herself who still hadn't grown accustomed to the American way of life; to the familiarity these people felt with one another almost immediately, with their desire to smile broadly even when there appeared to be no reason for it; to the closeness they felt even with virtual strangers, comfortable enough to reveal their own deepest desires and resentments.

Nathalie knew that she came off somewhat distant, maybe even aloof. She was what her fellow scientists described as a "hotshot" scientist, unafraid to experiment where others did not dare to go. That sense of adventure could also be seen in her apparel. Instead of wearing lab coats, she preferred clothing in dark shades, which clung to her buxom figure and matched her long black hair. Most of the other students worked, or had worked, in order to afford their tuition at the university, and frugality showed on their persons. They wore suits beneath their lab coats, just like their professors, but those outfits were well worn, frayed around the sleeves and cuffs. And while they tried to keep their hair and beards neatly trimmed, occasionally they resorted to homemade haircuts between the few professional ones. Nathalie, however, liked to be well groomed, and she never skimped on those luxuries, even if it meant doing without something else.

The other scientists found her clothes and demeanor a little strange, her refusal to give up her femininity in favor of white lab coats a bit eccentric. Why couldn't women be simply scientists, she often asked herself, without having to be judged for what they wore or how they looked? Why did they need to be called "women scientists"? Nathalie noticed that her peers in the laboratory were not described as "male scientists."

She sometimes told those closest to her that she got along better with dogs, of which she owned several. She spoke French to them, and they obeyed her commands only when addressed in that language. When visitors met the animals, they were startled to hear Nathalie speaking what sounded like gibberish in a language only her dogs understood. She had developed the same style of speaking even in the laboratory, French mingled with accented English.

She did not believe, as others did, that science was cold and calculating and that it required a similar disposition to practice it. Nor did she believe that she needed to abandon her likes and adopt those of her male colleagues in order to do her job well. She did not care whether or not they agreed with her, whether or not they liked her. She was not there to please them.

She knew that her coworkers paid too much attention to her outward appearance. However, the reality was that without Nathalie's development of the aluminum coating for the uranium slugs required by the Hanford reactors in Washington State, plutonium production would have stopped. But later, after the project was finished and her colleagues were asked about her, it was her long black hair that they remembered. Her Parisian clothing seemed to be the thing her peers concentrated on, and her hair and aristocratic manners seemed to have irked her coworkers more than anything else about her. No one seemed to recall her contributions at Hanford.

Although she was born in Russia, Nathalie had moved to Paris as a young girl with her mother to escape the Russian Revolution. She received her degree from the University of Paris in 1935, followed by a PhD in physical chemistry in 1939, at the age of thirty-two, with a concentration on the corrosion of metals. She later served as chief of metallurgy for the French Air Ministry. Nathalie and her mother left Paris when Hitler occupied France, landing in the United

States. She had feared that in the United States her skills would go unrecognized and instead she would have to settle for a position as a domestic or, worse, as a nanny: She did not get along with children, nor did she like them much.

But after working in the private sector for a while, she was hired for government work and sent to Chicago, where she advanced a project on preventing the corrosion of the aluminum that surrounded the uranium fuel in the pluto-nium production reactor. She didn't know how she had come to the government's attention, but she suspected Fermi, known in the laboratory as the "Benevolent Dictator," had something to do with it. She never asked him about it but felt that the two shared a secret no one else needed to know.

And now Nathalie watched silently as Leona was given the task of designing the project's first nuclear reactor (she would go on to be the only woman on the team that designed and built the Chicago Pile-1, the world's first nuclear reac-tor). But they would not be entirely her designs; she would use as models those of another physicist, Katharine "Kay" Way, who had found her way into the project in much the same way Leona had.

On receiving notice via telegram, Katharine "Kay" Way hopped into her car and headed to Chicago. The five-hundred-mile ride from Tennessee to Chicago seemed long in her wreck of a car, which she had purchased from a friend for less than two hundred dollars. She could hardly contain her excitement. The telegram she'd received had informed her that the engineers on the Manhattan Project planned to use her designs to build the nuclear reactors, a phenomenal outcome for an audacious young woman like herself.

She had come to their attention because she had made sure of it. Unlike the many other scientists who had been pursued by the project's officials, she had to nearly beg for a spot on the staff. But that was just like everything else Kay did. A runt, people called her, one who had to weasel her way into every opportunity. Even though that was the impression she gave others, the reality was much different. She worked hard for every break she got, and when hard work wasn't enough, a little finagling made the difference.

Kay was a graduate of Vassar College and Columbia University, where she had studied mathematics and physics, along with European languages. She had received her PhD in physics from the University of North Carolina at Chapel Hill, where she had been John Wheeler's (a theoretical physicist and former colleague of Niels Bohr) first graduate student in nuclear physics before she was hired as an assistant professor by the University of Tennessee. It was there that she heard rumors traversing the hallways of a secret government project that was under way, and kept vigilant for any new developments.

During her free time, she spent hours in the laboratory, where lately she had been interested in the construction of neutron sources, which produced neptunium-239. In 1942, she received an invitation to go to Washington to work with John Bardeen, who would later win two Nobel Prizes in Physics.

It was from Bardeen that she received in-depth information on the nuclear project, especially on the facility located in Chicago. She began to write letters to everyone she knew and anyone who could help her, and given the need for physicists, she was quickly interviewed and hired.

As she rumbled down the crooked roads from Tennessee to Chicago, ready and eager to do her part, she mused on how far she had come. They would use her designs to build the reactors, which could, in theory, make a difference in how the war turned out.

Sure, she had been told that she was going to collaborate with others, including a young woman named Leona, who, she had been warned, had a tendency for taking charge of everything. But overall, this would be her project, with her designs, despite what anyone else tried to do. How proud she would feel going down in history, Kay later wrote; she had always yearned to do something different from her peers, and now it would happen. How exciting it would be to be known by everyone one day, for something that no man had been able to accomplish.

chapter thirteen

The Reactor

Joan Hinton arrived in Los Alamos in the spring of 1944, tired and hungry. Hot, too. She entered 109 East Palace, the spot she had been instructed to go to await further instructions. This was the location that served not only as a reception venue but also as an information and traveling center. It also served snacks, something Joan appreciated, especially at that moment. There she would also find out how to finish her trip. As she read the instructions, a shiver ran down her spine. It was so thrilling, so exciting, this new adventure of hers—straight out of a spy novel, it seemed to her.

Dotty McKibben greeted the new arrivals every day as they entered 109 East Palace and listened as they bombarded her with a slew of questions. The forty-five-year-old single mother had grown used to the inquiries, which were always the same, varying only in degrees of fatigue and frustration: Where should they go to now? How should they get there? Did they serve food anywhere around here? Where could they find a snack or a cold beverage? After answering their questions, Dotty doled out security passes and instructions, including the ones that told the scientists that, from now on, their new address would be PO Box 1663 and that advised them to refrain from calling one another by their professional titles and to refer to themselves only by their new given name.

Much like the rest, Joan arrived there breathless and sweaty, tired from having slept little on the journey, the trains being slow, crowded, loud, and hot. She felt sticky all over and very drowsy. She wanted to curl up on a bench outside the office and rest. Instead, she was handed a yellow map that had been specifically prepared for the new arrivals and upon which several important points had been marked in red pencil. Then she waited for her ride, which would drive her to Los Alamos through scrappy roads and high mountains.

Scientists, their families, and all other required personnel had started to move into the area in fall 1943, some five or six months before Joan arrived. All of them were stunned by the seclusion of the place. In fact, their nearest neighbors were the Indian pueblos of San Ildefonso and Santa Clara, some fifteen or twenty miles away. Santa Fe was about thirty miles to the southeast, and to reach it they had to cross the Rio Grande, a river that for many brought to mind cascades of water but in reality for most of the year was just a puny little trickle, as most of its waters were used for irrigation.

The community had quickly mushroomed like a desert mirage. In a matter of months, a whole city had been set up; it soon began to welcome thousands of new residents to the area. Those living in the surrounding mountain abodes didn't know what the newcomers were doing. The new arrivals were not the friendliest people, locals thought, not to mention that many of them spoke with strong foreign accents. They wore casual rumpled clothes, shoes that were worn and dusty, and gave the impression of being too mellow. Wouldn't they go about in suits if they were doing something important?

The inhabitants of northern New Mexico often wondered what was happening inside the facility. Maybe they were working for the Russians, some distrustful fellows whispered over cups of coffee, or building a submarine or two. Others, having noticed members of the Women's Army Corps walking about, suspected that the compound was a home for pregnant members of that unit; the pregnant women were brought there to await the birth of their illegitimate children, they surmised, then taken away.

J. Robert Oppenheimer was aware of the gossip that circulated around Los Alamos and realized that it was getting wilder by the minute. Still, he suspected that within those rumors someone would eventually land on the truth, and when that person did, there would be trouble. It seemed to him that the best way to counteract such a threat was to dispatch some fabrication of their own, a credible story that would sound much like a truth. He ordered various members of the team who were known to enjoy spending time in the local bars and cafés or shopping around town to somehow let it slip that in the laboratories they were actually building electric rockets. He knew this would make the rounds and eventually all the inhabitants in the area would start talking about it. However, he also advised his people to be wary of those who asked too many questions, for there might be spies lurking within the compound, too.

The locals did not know precisely who Oppenheimer was or what he did, but they got accustomed to seeing him ride his chestnut mare along the trails to the west of Los Alamos, and sometimes even in town, smiling and waving and tipping his hat to those he passed by.

As soon as Joan got to Los Alamos, she was warned to be careful about what she said and about the things she asked.

She hadn't needed much encouragement to travel to New Mexico. Her family and friends wouldn't know where she was, and she couldn't tell them. They would not know what kind of project she was working on, and if she suddenly felt the need to unburden herself, if doubts about her work crept in, she wouldn't be able to reveal any of them. She also didn't know how long she would be required to be in Los Alamos. The war, the conflict, could go on indefinitely; they had no final date for completing the project. It could be a handful of months, or it could be years.

The fence, everybody knew, had been erected for two purposes: to keep nosy neighbors out and to keep employees in. It had the desired effect. No outsiders ever tried to break in, curious as they probably were. And, symbolically, it isolated the scientists, their families, and everybody else who worked within the compound from the rest of the community. It set them apart. Los Alamos became a world unto itself, where no one could go in or out without a specific purpose or permission from someone else; they even needed a pass to leave the premises for fun.

When Joan Hinton first approached the houses that had been built, they did not impress her. They looked like the tenement houses in the slums of major cities she had read about in books but never visited. Dispirited, she felt her initial excitement fade. There was laundry hanging everywhere on clotheslines stretching from fence to fence in small backyards. Garbage cans overflowed on the streets and in front yards. Dust from the roads coated cars, baby strollers, toys, front steps, and facades; even the people often went around covered in dust. They were hideous, these homes, even though people assured Joan that inside they were not as bad as they looked. She did not believe them.

The houses were adorned with couches, chairs, tables, and cots, but the living conditions were spartan, the bare essentials made up of military furniture that was neither good-looking nor comfortable. She woke each morning more tired than when she went to bed, the cot hard, tough, and itchy on her back.

The town had grown fast, and while at first there might have been some kind of plan for its construction, builders eventually did what they wanted with the design, so that in time it looked haphazard, without any order to its general look. In its so-called center was Ashley Pond, which was really not a pond but a little pool of water. In winter, the pond was used for ice-skating, while in the summer, people took advantage of its waters for swimming. On one side of this pond stood the laboratories, and on the other was the hospital. Opposite that were eight rows of ugly green barracks, which housed army personnel, and to the east were duplexes.

The laboratory had an array of charts, blackboards, maps, and equations in various states of development. It was actually a group of laboratories, collectively known as the Technical Area, or Tech Area, directed by Oppenheimer. Arthur Compton, as the leader of a small group of theoreticians who would be studying the bomb's detonation capabilities, had originally proposed Oppenheimer for a job. But General Leslie Groves, not particularly fond of Compton and enthralled by Oppenheimer's ideas, instead had promoted Oppenheimer as the head of the entire bomb design project, in July 1943, in essence, taking the job away from Compton. It was a blow to Compton, given that he had spearheaded the success of the very first chain reaction in Chicago.

In July 1943, the Office of Scientific Research and Development, upon the request by General Groves, granted security clearance to Oppenheimer to become full director of the Los Alamos National Laboratory. Up until that point, Oppenheimer had no practical experience in administration. It was an odd choice; as many of those who knew him from his Berkeley days had said, at one point or another, that "he couldn't run a hamburger stand."

Oppenheimer was young and brilliant, a product of the University of California, and he did not like secrets among the scientists. He often instructed those who worked for him to share their work, and his, with one another. He believed they could benefit from a free exchange of ideas, bouncing their theories off each other. He went so far as to hold weekly informal meetings where they all debated the merits of what they were working on. Aside from the sharing of ideas, this type of environment helped with everyone's morale. They also looked over one another's work for mistakes, of which they found very few.

Leona had once met Oppenheimer at the Institute for Advanced Study at Princeton University. She had not particularly liked him, and that feeling carried over when she met him again in Los Alamos. She thought him "an accomplished actor," a charismatic man who played his cards right. She would watch as he charmed others into following him, and his ideas benefited from the relationship he had developed with General Groves.

While Leona thought Oppenheimer was a dedicated and gifted teacher, she never fell under his spell. She found it puzzling, and a little disturbing, how his students, and even some of his coworkers, went so far as to copy his gestures, the way he spoke, and even the way he thought, as if in doing so they could come close to greatness. She knew that he could influence others greatly, and she feared that.

She thought it odd that he always managed to ask a lot of questions, to elicit a lot of information from his peers and devotees, yet hardly ever gave a response himself. His method of teaching was to instigate complicated trains of thought, which he wanted others to unravel. She suspected that perhaps he had the answers already but wanted to give others the opportunity to reach the conclusions themselves.

The tensions within the Tech Area, when there were any, normally came to the forefront when General Groves visited. With his bombastic personality, he took the brunt of the scientists' frustration. For his part, General Groves did not understand the scientists and made no effort to learn about them. His dismissive attitude toward their problems made him come across as naive about the sciences at best, crude and vulgar at worst. Often the squabbling became so ferocious that Oppenheimer had to put himself in the middle to stop it.

The Technical Area could be entered only if one wore

a white, pink, or green badge, and it was heavily guarded. Upon arrival, Joan was given security clearance and also a pink badge, which gave her access to a few other restricted areas of Los Alamos. Here worked the scientists, the chemists, the metallurgists, the other experts in their fields, some of whom remained on the premises all day long and well into the night. Army cots were set up against the walls, and Joan learned that some of the men hardly ever went home, doing so only occasionally to shower and change and to kiss their wives and children hello.

"The laboratories had a cluttered, disorderly, academic air. The offices were simple enough, though incredibly dirty, overcrowded, and badly equipped," said Charlotte Serber, who worked there as a technical librarian. "Physically, the Tech Area was certainly not a very unusual place. But it did have a spirit which was strange. Its tempo was too fast; its excitement was almost too high. The area was in a state of continuous crisis, and it soon became clear that speedup was its permanent tempo and excitement its permanent mood. The hyperthyroid quality was contagious and soon, in each newcomer to the Area, any disappointment with its physical drabness, was rapidly followed by a real enthusiasm for both its work and its personnel." The pace was so fast, there seemed to be no time to catch one's breath.

There was no general sense of unease among the scientists about what they were doing. Maybe doubts crept in once they left the laboratories and returned home, but within their work compounds, for the most part, there was only a feeling of urgency; they needed to finish the project as soon as possible. Any day that passed, any hour that went by without progress, brought the Germans closer to their own finished product. What if the Germans unleashed the bomb first?

Despite the importance of the work that went on there, Los Alamos was an informal place, and most people liked the casual feel of it and the fact that no one cared to dress up or to shine their shoes. No one bothered with titles or formalities, and nicknames abounded.

Joan was surprised to see so many women at Los Alamos, as she had been told that only a few female scientists, like herself, had been hired. Only later did she understand that most of the women were not scientists; they were there in other capacities. She later read a quote by General Groves: "This system was designed to encourage the wives of our people to work on the project, for those who worked obtained priority on household assistance. Some of the wives were scientists in their own right, and they, of course, were in great demand. But," he said, "with labor at a premium we could put to good use everyone we could get, whether as secretaries or as technical assistants or as teachers in the public school that we started for the children."

Joan Hinton was told she would be assisting Enrico Fermi, and soon thereafter she was assigned to work with his group on the high-power (HYPO) reactor. One morning, as she entered the lab, someone whispered to her, "The plutonium has come. It's in a little room. It feels warm to the touch."

Handling plutonium was a risky business. Working with it in the water boiler was dangerous, mostly because of the properties of the reactor, particularly the high radioactivity level; but there was also the possibility of a meltdown. Furthermore, the scientists were not very familiar with plutonium. It was still a relatively new discovery, and they dealt with it haphazardly, largely unaware of the damage it could cause.

Although Joan had been warned not to do so, she cautiously stole into the next room to look at the plutonium when no one else was around. She didn't dare touch it, but she stood there a moment, marveling at its awesome power. It stunned her that something so small could apply such force. The substance was about the size of a baseball and as malleable as soft cheese. It was toxic to inhale, though the scientists working alongside her seemed oblivious to such details. She stared at the plutonium for a moment, then walked away, smiling. She now knew that they were almost ready.

All the researchers were excited when the first few small quantities of plutonium arrived at Los Alamos, even if they had received only a fraction of what they needed. Then, at the start of 1944, additional grams of plutonium began arriving with more regularity, first from Oak Ridge, Tennessee, and then from Hanford, Washington.

Joan Hinton learned that Fermi had two groups of scientists working at Los Alamos. The first group was made up of theoretical physicists who also performed experiments. The second group seemed a little more interesting to her, and it was to this group that she was assigned. The members were appointed to work in a canyon some distance away from the main facility. They were charged with building one of the first reactors that would use enriched uranium for fuel. As it turned out, they built two reactors as testing sites, one for uranium and one for plutonium.

They were isolated from the rest of the group, and Joan suspected that this was done on purpose. In case an accident occurred, only those in the one group would be involved, only they would be hurt.

Her job was to help with the design and construction of the central rods. However, she also assisted with the piling of beryllium blocks around the physical core and manufacturing the electronic circuit.

They lived on the edge, and Joan was aware of that; it was exciting, perilous, and frightening in many ways. Before this, scientists had worked with only very small amounts of radioactive materials, whereas the Manhattan Project required the handling of huge stores of uranium and plutonium. How would coming so close to these materials affect the body? In very small doses, plutonium was not extremely dangerous, but what if someone got irradiated by a large dose? What would that do to the body? Could one survive? The scientists were experimenting with elements they had never practiced with before; if an accident occurred, they did not know if they would be capable of handling it. And on more than one occasion that became painfully obvious.

Not long after arriving, a colleague of Joan's, Harry Daghlian, left the canyon for the laboratory located inside the facility there to perform an elaborate and detailed experiment: He was to measure the critical mass of uranium. But something went awry, and his hands were immediately irradiated. Joan heard the urgent screams as she entered the laboratory. Harry Daghlian was rushed to the hospital, and for the next three weeks his limbs turned gray and wasted, and he soon descended into a slow, painful death that Joan had not even considered possible before coming to Los Alamos.

The accident left an indelible mark on her, as it did on everyone who knew him. It was then that the questions began. If a small amount of radiation had caused such an outcome on one individual, what would an atomic bomb do when dropped on a country where millions of people lived? How many would die right away, and how many would suffer the effects afterward? How many would survive the blast without any actual effects? And they were building two bombs in Los Alamos, which meant twice the number of victims.

It finally became clear to officials that as the project

progressed, all the workers would be dealing not only with new substances but also with huge amounts of radioactivity, the likes of which they had never come across before. Given the possibilities, new medical limits had to be implemented to ensure safety. The health of the workers became of paramount importance, much as reaching their goal did, and the Manhattan Project Medical Section was therefore established. This section not only doled out medical care but also conducted safety drills and coordinated biomedical research between the sites and the universities associated with the project. Their goal was to study radiation and its long-term effects on the individual, as well as to prevent any experiments from becoming too dangerous.

The doctors in the medical section routinely examined the fingertips of those scientists who worked with the radioactive substances, as that was the first area to show physical changes. If any serious accidents occurred or following prolonged exposured to radiation, they immediately tested blood and urine samples. They also treated ordinary medical problems. Each of the sites had its own medical section that dealt with everyday concerns, particularly those of the children who lived on the bases.

In Los Alamos, Enrico Fermi had traded his hours swimming in Lake Michigan for hours spent hiking in the local mountains. Always accompanying him was a big, burly Italian American bodyguard who could hardly keep up the pace. He was often heard complaining, as he would have preferred going up on a horse, particularly when the hike involved heading up toward Lake Peak. However, soon enough, the bodyguard got the relief he yearned for when someone else replaced him: Joan Hinton became a confidante to Enrico Fermi. She began joining him on his walks and showed off her skiing expertise going down the slopes next to the famous physicist. And she played violin in Fermi's quartet, which also included Edward Teller.

It certainly was, Joan later mused, the experience of a lifetime, work more interesting than anything she had ever imagined she would find when she'd enrolled at the university. As the days rolled by, she reckoned that she might stay for the duration of the project, even if the seclusion and the secrecy of it were getting to her. Perhaps, if things were good after the bomb project ended, the Manhattan Project might continue and ask her to stay longer. She thought she might say yes.

chapter fourteen

Diz

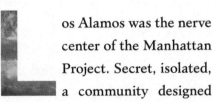os Alamos was the nerve center of the Manhattan Project. Secret, isolated, a community designed to be self-sustaining located at an altitude of around 7,500 feet, it had been built from the ground up deep in the Jemez Mountains of north-central New Mexico. It was to there that some of the greatest American and European scientific minds were spirited away to work on the atomic bomb. It was a strange notion, at once exciting and frightening, to have all this intellectual power collected at one spot to bring to life an atomic bomb.

When officials started searching for a perfect site on which to create the bomb, they knew it had to have certain conditions: The weather had to be temperate, even in winter.

It had to be close to a railroad station and to an airport, so that people could easily access it. But it also had to possess a certain measure of remoteness and be only sparsely populated, so that guards could fend off the curious.

The New Mexico location took its name from the Los Alamos Ranch School for Boys, a former exclusive private school whose facilities were now occupied by the military, which had also taken over Fuller Lodge—still being used as it had been before, as a dining space serving mediocre food. What remained of the school's halls and rooms became a small shop and some additional residences. There were actually two shops on the premises, neither of which offered anything worth indulging in. If one happened to be in the mood for warm Coca-Cola and an assortment of sandwiches featuring limp deli meats and day-old egg salad, well, those were the places to be. But they had a jukebox, and music was always a welcome reprieve.

When the United States Army took over the area, at the start of the Manhattan Project, it also took over the nearby ranches, where it built laboratories and testing facilities. Here the scientists tackled unanswered questions and worked on mysterious, puzzle-like projects. Upon arriving, most of them felt like children running free within a candy store, the only difference here being that their results could have catastrophic outcomes for everyone involved.

It did not take long for Joan Hinton to sense that working at the facility would be a challenge. The project required discretion, she was warned often. Even though there weren't many outsiders to whom she and the others could divulge any information, she was told that secrecy was of the utmost importance at Los Alamos.

In addition, they had to report all their movements, however minor, to the Los Alamos officials: whether they were going into town for shopping or for pleasure, and whom they met along the way. Clearance was required to leave Los Alamos, and questions, almost similar to those at an inquisition, were asked of anyone whom they happened to bump into and talk with.

The laboratories were located above a mesa, some thirty miles from Santa Fe, and painted a bilious green color. One reached Los Alamos through a treacherous road that ran along the San Ildefonso Mountains and over the Rio Grande, which could be muddy and brown, at once tumultuous or a mere trickle, depending on the weather and its temperament. Still, the view was stunning as people drove up toward the mesa, with the Sangre de Cristo Mountains as the backdrop. Some made it a point to arrive at sunset to watch the color palette change in ways they had never seen before—a blend of various shades of pink, orange, scarlet, and lavender. The pink shades reminded many new arrivals of salmon, and made a few recall youthful fishing trips with their parents and grandparents. Below it was the desert plain, a rusty color varnished by the winds, smooth and flat.

Before anyone could enter Los Alamos, the military police guards who manned the gate stopped them. Everything was inspected. The guardhouse was small, but it did the trick, sheltering those on duty from the elements, whether sun, wind, rain, or the occasional dust storm. It was painted the same ugly shade of green as the laboratories, the color giving the newly arrived a preview of what they could expect on the inside.

The location was so remote, enveloped in such an oppressive hush-hush atmosphere, that Joan hardly ever saw anyone who didn't belong there. And that could play havoc with the mind, Elizabeth Graves, the physicist she met soon after arriving, told her—especially if one yearned for friends and companions. Joan also learned that there was a housing shortage, services were limited, and there was no entertainment to speak of. Still, much like Elizabeth, most of the new arrivals were happy and excited to be there, to be working on a project that promised to end the war.

Elizabeth Graves went by the nickname of Diz. She had married Al Graves when they were both graduate students in physics at the University of Chicago. After completing his PhD, Al had accepted a faculty position at the University of Texas at Austin, where Diz thought she would be teaching, too. But despite her PhD in nuclear physics from the University of Chicago, the University of Texas refused to hire her, citing their strict nepotism rules. However, Diz knew that was just an excuse: The head of the physics department at UT Austin had a less than positive view of the new crop of female physicists, and of women in science in general, often expressing his opinion of where women should remain: in the bedroom and in the kitchen. Diz had sent a strongly worded letter expressing her opinions to the department and the institution, but it was ignored.

Diz's parents hadn't wanted her to pursue her scientific ambitions, either, her mother preferring that she go after a teaching degree and her father that she find herself a husband. But from the start, Diz had no intention of fitting into the passive role expected of women at the time.

Diz's research was considered top-notch. Her PhD dissertation, which she had completed at the University of Chicago while Fermi was there, involved neutron-scattering experiments, and this work had, of course, come to the attention of the Manhattan Project's officials, who quickly hired her to work on the selection of a neutron reflector surrounding the core of the atomic bomb. Once she and Al arrived at Los Alamos, they managed to ingratiate themselves into the community, most especially with Oppenheimer. And it was there that she pioneered a method to speed up the explosive growth of the chain reaction that powered the bomb.

As she worked on her experiments, she felt very removed from her university days, when she was just a girl crossing the halls of the University of Chicago, one of the few women in the physics department. She often reflected about how far she had come, further than her parents had ever imagined, further than they had ever wished for her.

chapter fifteen

The Professor
and the Apprentice

nitially, Leona Woods did not realize the impact Fermi would have on her life, either on a professional level or on a scientific one. At the Met Lab in Chicago, he taught her not only the scientific theories that would propel her to become one of the most important figures of the Manhattan Project but also the essence of how to deal with the other scientists, how to move along with scientific changes, and how to handle the humiliations that were part of everyday living inside the laboratories. She became an assistant, a colleague, and a friend.

Although she was a self-confident young woman, when she started working with Fermi and his colleagues she suffered a momentary bout of self-doubt, especially when she began associating with them on a more informal level, something Fermi wanted her to do. They often played the game Murder, and at one point she observed, "I shrank into the corner and listened with astonishment to these brilliant, accomplished, famous, sophisticated people shrieking and poking and kissing each other in the dark like little kids." They surprised her and they amused her. But they also appeared a little more human.

She soon discovered that Fermi did not believe, as most Americans did, that people were born with equal mental abilities. He had worked with a wide variety of personalities, he told her one day, and had noticed how different people were at a fundamental level. There were internal differences, he'd learned, no matter how hard people tried to pretend otherwise. The idea that anyone could become anything they wished if they simply tried hard enough, he imagined to be only wishful thinking, perhaps an American invention to give hope to those who had none. No amount of hard work would allow a person to become anything more than their nature had set them up to be. The predisposition for greatness usually showed up early on. As it had in him, he was not too humble to add.

Leona herself was not a humble young woman. She had realized from a young age that her intellect was exceptional and that it separated her from her peers. Listening to Enrico Fermi and his theories on greatness, she was often struck by the feeling that he might be correct.

Both Leona and Fermi were friends with Herbert Anderson, and it was Herbert who had helped solidify their friendship outside the laboratory. Soon after she started working at the lab, Leona began to spend time with Anderson and Fermi after work. Each evening, they escaped their laboratories and headed outside. Fermi was a powerful swimmer, whose notion of a good time included a few laps in the waters of Lake Michigan. This was usually done every day between five and six o'clock. She swam with them during the spring and summer, but when the colder weather arrived, she had a hard time keeping up with Fermi. So did his wife, Laura, who disliked the activity. He'd jump off the rocks from Promontory Point, swim a few laps, then walk back to the laboratory, accompanied by Anderson.

Fermi had initially arrived in Chicago without his wife and children, who were then settled in New Jersey. He had found housing for a short while in an apartment just around the corner from International House, where several professors and quite a few students, including Leona, were then living.

Eventually Laura Fermi joined her husband in September 1942, bringing along their children, Nella and Giulio. They rented a large house on University Avenue, and the children were soon enrolled in school, where they thrived, to Fermi's obvious delight. Greatness, he told Leona, was also hereditary.

Sometimes their swims in the lake were followed by the

large meals Laura would always prepare. It was during these suppers that Leona learned about the Fermis' life in Italy and about their leaving Rome. Their home in New Jersey had been bought with a portion of the Nobel Prize money, chosen because it possessed a big basement. Fermi had dug a deep hole in the basement floor and buried a good chunk of what was left of their savings. He had come to fear that now, because they were considered enemy aliens, someone might come in the middle of the night and take away what they owned or kick them out of the country that had so graciously welcomed them. Fear had pursued him in Italy, and while he was not as afraid in the United States, anxiety had now become a part of his persona.

While Fermi was an exceptional instructor at the university, he was first and foremost a physicist. He went nowhere without his slide rule, which he kept at the ready safely tucked in his breast pocket, his mind seemingly spinning a hundred ideas per minute. He had an office where he liked to work on his theories, initially doing so on his own, then sharing the results with his colleagues. When Leona joined the team, he got into the habit of calling on her in her tiny office, not far from his, to come join him, and together they pored over the day's calculations. It was not unusual for them to stay up late talking physics and performing experiments. Sharpened pencil in hand, or with screeching chalk on a blackboard, Leona probably spent more hours with him than his wife did.

He loved the United States, Fermi often told Leona, but he worried about his wife. He had wanted to leave Italy for some time, but it was only when he won the Nobel Prize that the opportunity to do so had presented itself. And Columbia University had stepped up. While he had been happy for the chance at a new life, Laura had not been happy about leaving Rome. She had a large family in Italy and an equally large group of friends. She loved Rome, which she believed was the center of the world, the Eternal City, with the most fascinating, wonderful people. It had not helped Fermi's cause that Laura came from a privileged family that had always provided for and doted on her. It was only the threat on their lives that had finally pushed her to agree to leave.

Laura had been a student at the University of Rome, where she studied electrical engineering. But after meeting Enrico, she gave up on those endeavors for the sake of marriage. And she never regretted it.

Those who came to know Laura Fermi in America wondered why she had bothered with a university course at all. She never asked her husband's colleagues any questions, nor did she seem interested in her husband's work or the projects that he was involved in at the University of Chicago. She didn't talk about politics or the war in Europe. Her conversations revolved around the children, their schoolwork and afternoon activities, food, olive oil, and good wine. While that was the impression she liked to give, in reality she was a deep thinker, as people would eventually find out—a woman who kept her feelings to herself rather than divulge them to others in the way she had come to expect from most Americans.

Fermi was a busy man and had the habit of withdrawing completely when working out a problem, holing up in his office and hardly communicating with anybody until he had cracked the answer. Taking little notice of anyone around him, he barely ate or drank, and Laura Fermi was aware of this. She let him be.

Laura had learned English at a very young age, so that when she arrived in the United States she spoke the language better than her husband did, a matter that irritated Fermi, as for a time he had difficulty communicating, and people complained of not being able to understand him.

Enrico had discovered the field of radioactivity in summer 1919, at the age of seventeen, when he read the laboratory notes of physician Ernest Rutherford. He wrote summaries of Rutherford's papers in his notebooks and studied them in depth, soon realizing that in Italy the subject was hardly ever discussed. By the time Fermi was twenty, he could also read scientific papers in German, which was very useful, given that much of the work in radioactivity was being done in Germany. He attended the graduate program at Pisa and in 1926 took part in a competition for a professorship being held by the University of Rome. He won, thus becoming the youngest professor the university had ever had.

His own experiments on the bombardment of matter

with neutrons started in 1934. Those experiments were performed alongside his students and colleagues, and he published dozens of articles about them. But the experiments ended when his Rome laboratory broke up and he moved to the United States, his colleagues scattering across Europe. However, he still hoped to carry on that work in America, he initially told Leona while working in Chicago, together with his new faithful associates.

chapter sixteen

Chicago Pile-1

I n scientific circles in the United States and the world over, not all scientists were thrilled with the idea of using science as a means for developing a bomb. Many hoped that some sort of technical glitch would prevent a chain reaction from happening, and in turn would prevent the building of an atomic weapon. But Enrico Fermi wished the opposite, and one night in December 1942, he conducted an experiment beneath the stands of the University of Chicago's stadium to prove once and for all that it could be done, that his hopes could be realized.

Arthur Compton had originally wanted the test to take place in an area about twenty miles southwest of Chicago, in the Argonne Forest, named for the Forest of Argonne in

France, where the United States troops had fought during World War I. The forest was heavily wooded with oak trees and had a log cabin that had once housed a Girl Scout club. The site was a pretty one, with trees flanking a lake that iced over in the winter; colorful flowers shooting up from the ground every spring and summer; and foliage changing hues as the summer days ended. Construction for the experiment started in earnest and continued at a frantic pace. However, by the time the scientists had collected enough graphite and uranium for the chain reaction, construction had not been completed. This posed a problem, as speed and efficiency were required. So it was decided that the experiment should be tried a little closer to home. The University of Chicago's Stagg Field was chosen as the spot; its stands, in the under-belly of the stadium, would have to work.

Compton agreed that Stagg Field's double squash court would be a suitable site. Despite its being in the middle of a stadium at the University of Chicago, and the university itself being in the center of a populated area, they did not expect trouble. Compton initially wondered if they should ask the president of the university for permission, but he didn't think it was necessary. No one, aside from them, needed to know about their doings.

On November 4, they prepared the double squash court under the west stands of Stagg Field. The layers of the graph-ite matrix were to be the supporting graphite for four- by six-inch timbers, which were carefully laid out. They performed this work very slowly and carefully, and by November 20, they had added a fifteenth layer of graphite.

Within each layer a hole was left for a zip rod, a long wooden stick wrapped in cadmium that would absorb neutrons. The rod was meant to be pulled out and dropped in with the help of a rope. If the rope snapped, the rod would fall and stop the chain reaction. If the rod was pulled out and held for a moment just before the pile started up again, or if it was let go, gravity would do the job and the rod would fall back into the pile. Walter Zinn, another scientist in Fermi's laboratory, was in charge of this whole operation, and he felt the weight of responsibility.

In addition to the zip rod, another wooden stick encased in cadmium had been added that could be manipulated by hand. There was an emergency bell that would ring if the boron trifluoride counters and ion chambers rose to a potentially dangerous level.

The morning of the test was frigid. Leona and Fermi stepped outside the slightly snow-covered grounds of the university buildings and onto the field, icy particles crunching beneath their feet. She held on to a thick pile of papers with Fermi's calculations and plans depicting the experiments reaching the critical points. Everything had been well thought out, with each person knowing his or her assignments. They made sure to have nearby a vat of concentrated nitrate solution, which could be used to douse the graphite pile in case of emergency, stopping the chain reaction. However, despite all their preparations, they felt agitated, as they knew that if the experiment worked, the repercussions would be historic.

Everyone was there as Leona, in a fairly loud voice, began to read the counts of the boron trifluoride counter: "Two, two, three, one." It was the manner of counting Enrico Fermi had designated, in ten-second intervals, and which she had memorized.

No one spoke in the darkness. Leona could hear her own teeth chattering from the cold, although she guessed the rattling was also partly due to the excitement. There was nothing normal about the situation, and they knew it. To quiet their nerves, some of them counted backward.

George Weil, one of the scientists present, pulled out the last control rod, plucking it out foot by foot, as Fermi had instructed him to do. Fermi, at that particular moment, was on the stands above them, watching the whole operation and making additional calculations on the spot, while Leona kept watch on the monitors.

Those present felt their anxiety growing by the minute, until finally Walter Zinn released the rope, the rod falling into the reactor, and the control rod was pushed in, the intensity of the neutrons dropping quickly. The chain reaction was thus stopped. Then it was started again, and everything operated normally. December 2, 1942, would go down in history as the first time a chain reaction had occurred. Sure, the spark had been only enough to power a lightbulb, but that was not important. What was important was the fact that it had worked.

Leona had spent two months beneath the stands of Stagg Field preparing for the first chain reaction, and its success made her giddy. Fermi had instructed her to read everything she could about the latest developments on plutonium production reactors; she had also prepared the counters for the graphite piles. Now her work had come to fruition. She felt giddy with pride.

Leona and the others started locking every control mechanism and turning off the power supply. They were about to don their overcoats to walk back to the laboratories when Eugene Wigner, another scientist in the Fermi group, who was carrying a bottle of Chianti wine, stopped them. Given that Fermi was Italian, Wigner thought Chianti a fine choice to commemorate the occasion. He had also found some minuscule paper cups, and in those he managed to pour some wine for the nearly two dozen people present. Each person then signed his or her name on the bottle.

Eugene Wigner later wrote: "The success of the experiment, its accomplishment, had a deep impact on us. For some time we had known that we were about to unlock a giant; still, we could not escape an eerie feeling when we knew we had actually done it. We felt as, I presume, everyone feels who has done something he knows will have very far-reaching consequences which he cannot foresee."

Leona and Fermi returned to the university's laboratory,

their feet echoing loudly on the frozen ground, the temperature having dropped below zero. They said little. Leona didn't know what Fermi was thinking, and she didn't want to ask; however, she could speculate. She imagined his thoughts were just as heavy as hers. "Of course, the Germans have already made a chain reaction because we have," she told herself, "and they have been ahead until now. When do we get as scared as we ought to and work harder?" No one knew how far the Germans were in their own development of the bomb, but just like every other scientist, Leona feared that the Americans were falling behind. However, she didn't share these thoughts with Fermi. Arriving near the laboratory, they went their separate ways.

Completing the experiment beneath the stands at the University of Chicago had seemed like a good idea. Fermi had decided to use several neutron-absorbing cadmium rods. As he slowly inserted those into the pile, the fission chain reaction stopped. If he wanted to get it started again, he needed to pull out a rod again—this action was performed very, very slowly.

Of his success, Fermi had this to say: "The first pile had no device built in to remove the heat provided by the reaction, and it was not provided with any shield to absorb the radiations produced by the fission process. For these reasons, it could be operated only at the nominal power which never exceeded two hundred watts. [Two hundred watts will illuminate a couple of lightbulbs.] It proved, however, two points: that the chain reaction with graphite and natural uranium was possible, and that it was very easily controllable."

In mid-1942, Zinn and his assistants removed the graphite-and-uranium assembly from beneath the stands of Stagg Field and transferred them to the Argonne Forest, which was still a forested lot when they began dismantling the original pile. Along with the pile went pertinent instruments, pliers, files, and whatever else was needed or that Leona Woods had managed to steal from other departments.

The scientists felt a lot of pressure at Argonne. The new pile was now nicknamed CP-2; the new laboratory contained a large machine shop for construction, a chemistry shop for experiments, and a long room that worked as an office. The two-story dormitories were two wide-open spaces that were not used efficiently, Leona thought, as one was the domain of all the men involved in the project, and the other one was entirely her own, as she was the only woman on staff. Between the two dormitories was a bathroom with a shower and a toilet, which they all shared, to her despair. The men were not a tidy bunch, especially when they did their laundry and hung it in the bathroom. John Marshall made a habit of taking his damp underwear into Leona's dormitory, where there was more space. On the first floor of the dormitories were the offices of Enrico Fermi and Walter Zinn.

The Argonne Forest was part of the Cook County Forest Preserve and was managed by a forest ranger and a handful of guards who were less than thrilled with their jobs. But every evening they seemed to take pleasure in cleaning their shotguns, something they practiced with a delicacy that bordered on deference. On one occasion, one of the guards accidentally discharged a round of pellets toward the offices. Fortunately, no one was working at that moment.

Following her work at the Argonne Forest, Leona was sent to Hanford, Washington, to start up the plutonium production reactors.

Hanford was a small village located at a bend in the Columbia River, downriver from the Grand Coulee Dam. For many years it had served as a center for several ranchers who had built their homes along the Columbia's banks. The river and, more important, the dam, played a significant role in the government's decision to choose that spot to build the plutonium production reactors. The dam made available more than 300 megawatts of electricity to power the construction, the pumps, and the city that would eventually spring up around the facility. And the reactor's cooling systems required nearly 75,000 gallons of fresh water per minute, for which the Columbia River was ideally suited.

Surrounding the few ranches, there was only vastness, a great empty space. It would be no trouble at all, officials felt, to lease some 500,000 acres. And those few ranchers who would be displaced would move elsewhere.

When Leona arrived, she could see only empty land: the low hills across the Columbia River and, to the west, the foothills of Yakima Ridge, flanking the Cascade Range. There was an abundance of sagebrush, and she frequently spotted coyotes and rabbits. Sometimes she liked to watch flocks of geese as they flew across the Columbia and then returned at night—small dots speckling the sky.

Because such a vast desert surrounded Hanford, they were often plagued by sandstorms. The wind blew sand in their faces, covering their bodies, getting in their hair and eyes. Storms could last two or three days and had the power to halt production.

The project required not only scientists and engineers but also the help of hundreds, and eventually tens of thousands, of other workers. This gave job seekers from different walks of life the opportunity to be part of one of the most secret projects ever created. It was a mammoth operation. Pipefitters arrived daily, as did plumbers, bricklayers, canteen workers, and landscapers. Most of them were housed and worked in a camp made of temporary wood-framed buildings. The project brought extraordinary wealth to the area, as thousands of people arrived every day to work. By 1944, at the height of Hanford's activity, the workforce hovered around 51,000 people. And of those, nearly 10 percent were women.

The whole facility was built in a great hurry, the area bustling with carpenters, electricians, and everybody else arriving on the Northern Pacific Railroad. They mixed the sand and gravel already on the spot with cement and water to make concrete to build the reactor buildings, along the basins that would hold the cooling water. That water would stay there until the last trace of radioactivity was present, and then it would be dumped back into the Columbia River.

The first reactor at Hanford become known as the B Reactor, and it was completed and operating in September 1944. Around the same time, other plants were finished, too, such as the ones needed to extract plutonium from irradiated slugs. It took less than a year to complete construction for the entire Hanford operation, and what rose in the Washington State desert was a gigantic complex that functioned completely on its own by early 1945. And soon enough, Hanford was able to produce the amount of plutonium that was needed for the July 1945 Trinity test in New Mexico as well as for the Nagasaki bomb.

Enrico Fermi arrived at Hanford almost two weeks before the first plutonium reactor started up. When the time came to fuel up the large reactor, Leona and Fermi walked quietly around the control room, checking every knob, looking at graphs and charts, trying to appease bosses who had come in for the momentous occasion.

The slow, easy movement of pulling out the rods, step-by-step, one by one, began. It was not unlike the experiment back at Stagg Field. However, this was of a much larger scale, and the witnesses were the tough employers whose expectations were much greater: the military and the government. The reactor was performing as it should have.

Once again, all the scientists knew what they were supposed to be doing and went around the room controlling outlets, inspecting wires, taking readings, and talking to one another in whispers, as if fearing the reactors would hear them and decide to act capriciously.

But then something odd happened, and Leona appeared to be one of the last to find out that there was something wrong with the apparatus. The radioactivity in the pile was slowing down, decreasing beat by beat, which was not supposed to happen. Slowly, the power dropped, until it died down completely. The initial excitement in the control room was now gone, replaced by an overwhelming sense of doom. No one said anything for a few moments.

Leona had noticed the peculiar drop, she admitted to Fermi. It had been linear. Maybe a water leak had caused it and it wasn't necessarily anything to do with radioactivity. Fermi agreed to have some testing done, but he wanted to wait until the morning, as he suspected that the problem was not as grave as they thought.

Overnight, as one of the operators kept watch on the apparatus, he saw the pile restart and then go through the same process of shutting down just moments later. It repeated the operation a second time.

For several days, operators, scientists, technicians, electricians, engineers, and everyone else involved in the construction of the pile watched as the apparatus shut down on its own, then restarted again. They made calculations, looked at possibilities, and tried to figure out what could possibly be happening. Finally, Fermi calculated that if all the extra holes of the reactors were loaded with uranium slugs, the reactors would have enough radioactivity for a successful operation. As indeed it did. There was no more shutting down. The reactors performed successfully, producing the first patches of plutonium, which were then shipped off to Los Alamos, where the makings of the atomic bomb were already under way.

Leona Woods married John Marshall in July 1943 and soon thereafter became pregnant. She moved around the building in large overalls and oversized denim jackets, which were her usual work clothes. Her pockets often contained pens, papers, pliers, notebooks, and rulers, all of which provided additional bulk, and for months her colleagues did not realize that she was pregnant.

She arrived early in the morning by bus, one of those army-issued ones that had neither heat nor other comforts. It was painted blue for some reason, and the color made her queasy. It was not an easy trip, particularly for a pregnant woman. Her morning included the rough ride to the laboratory and a quick dash to the bathroom to vomit, and then she headed to her office to begin her day.

The laboratory was nearly thirty miles away from the hospital where she was planning to give birth. Fermi worried that she would not be able to reach medical help in time if her labor came on suddenly. Initially, he did not tell Leona, but he had asked his wife, Laura, about childbirth lessons, just in case he had to deliver Leona's baby himself. When Leona found out, she vowed that this would be an experiment he would not get to perform—something that she suspected he would be highly disappointed about. Neither one had to be worried. As it turned out, while at home one night she felt ill, her blood pressure spiked, and she was rushed to the hospital. Two days later, she left with a baby.

While in the hospital, she recalled a time when she and a coworker were irradiated with a large dose of gamma rays. Her white blood cells quickly dropped to half the normal level, although at the time she hadn't been worried; she had actually been more concerned with any leaks that might have occurred in the experiments. None had happened, and the work was later completed properly.

She had continued to feel tired for a while and sought medical aid from the doctors at the Met Lab. But rather than helping her, they had lectured her about the proper duties of a woman and how many egg cells a female possessed. Did Leona know that she had only a certain number of good eggs, and that they could be easily destroyed by the radiation? She would never be able to procreate if she went down this path, the doctors told her, adding that perhaps she should have chosen a different career. She was left feeling ashamed and dumbfounded. Even though her colleague Willard Libby was irradiated in the same incident, she later learned that he had not been lectured about his sperm count.

But now she had her baby, proof enough that the irradiation had caused her no harm.

Leona returned to work shortly after the birth of her son, as her mother was willing to help take care of the child, the household duties, and whatever else needed to be done to keep Leona's house running smoothly. The older woman practically ran Leona's domestic life, which Leona didn't mind. Her expertise was needed, she knew, and she was eager to get back to work.

chapter seventeen

The Los Alamos Visit

n 1945, Maria Goeppert-Mayer visited Los Alamos. She left her children with a nursemaid and did not tell Joseph Mayer where she was going or why. On arriving in New Mexico, she met with Laura Fermi, whose family had been living in Los Alamos since the summer of 1944.

Although she had not told her husband the reason for her trip, he sensed that his wife was involved in the development of the bomb, though he did not know to what extent. As much as he wanted to know, he was aware of the secret nature of the experiments and tried not to push her to disclose more than she was comfortable revealing. Joseph Mayer had also been invited to join the confidential project, but he had refused, unable to take the endeavor seriously.

He found the idea of building such a weapon ridiculous and did not want to become entangled in a project that would certainly end in failure, he told officials. However, Joseph did not know that Enrico Fermi had been able to operate the first atomic pile beneath the stands of the University of Chicago stadium. And he also did not know of the work happening at Oak Ridge or Hanford, much less at Los Alamos.

From Maria's point of view, it was a strain on her marriage to keep that secret from Joseph. She also feared for Germany and its people. She despised Adolf Hitler but loathed the idea of harm coming to the good people of her country.

As Maria traveled to Los Alamos and toured the facilities, she was overwhelmed with fear. She tried to pinpoint what that gnawing presentiment was about and realized that two factors were nagging her: She was worried that Hitler and his scientists had already advanced far enough in their designs and constructed a bomb; and she was also afraid that the Americans would soon succeed in building and detonating the bomb themselves. As a scientist, she wanted to see an experiment come to fruition; she wanted to see the work come to light. And yet, what would happen when it did? How many innocent lives would be lost because of their doings? And how many lives would be lost because of the doings of a madman?

Her internal conflict was originally ignited by loyalty to her mentors. Max Born, the man she had gone to when her father passed away, the man who had put aside his own inner demons to help her wrestle with hers, had refused to help the British in their atomic projects; and James Franck, her former professor, had raised loud questions about the morality of unleashing such a powerful bomb on innocent people. Few had listened to him.

She knew that her husband would be able to understand her sense of loyalty to her family and friends, to her nation, and, to a certain extent, to the good people who still existed in Germany. Yet she could not tell him. And she certainly could not tell her children. She felt torn. And that rip was destroying her.

chapter eighteen

Coming to America

lizabeth Rona was still in Europe. The finicky American immigration policies were not allowing her to travel, and she was becoming antsy.

US officials had already invited Elizabeth's friend Lise Meitner to visit Los Alamos to see how their work was progressing and what they were planning. They had nearly begged her to go. But Lise had declined. Officials knew she was unhappy in Sweden, and they had come to believe that time away from her current environment would be good for her, and for them. They had made many offers and tried to entice her with a terrific visiting schedule to Los Alamos, but she always said no. She knew that it was not out of generosity that the Americans had asked her to travel to the United

States, nor to simply look at their facilities; it was because they wanted her to work on the bomb.

The British delegation heading to Los Alamos also tried to persuade Lise to join them as their guest in New Mexico, but she had once again adamantly refused. "I will have nothing to do with a bomb," she told them, this time more firmly.

The idea that people could die because of something she had done weighed heavily on Lise, although it had not always been so. In fact, early in her career, morality had not even entered her mind. She could pinpoint the precise moment when she began to question a scientist's place in the grand scheme of things and her own responsibility toward others.

She recalled that day in Berlin. In 1914, World War I had broken out. Hahn had been called into the service by the German army, and within their circle he was no longer Professor Hahn but Lieutenant Hahn. One day, in full uniform, he had spoken at the Kaiser Wilhelm Institute for Chemistry to a group of scientists and professors, many of whom were about to leave the institute to perform their own military duties.

Lise appeared not to understand the gravity of the situation. "But why now?" she had asked Hahn. "Just when we've hit upon isotopes!" It struck some as an unusually selfish way to be looking at the outbreak of war, but then she had never been confronted with the possibility of war before.

She, too, would have to do her part, she was told. She was going to become an X-ray nurse with the Austro-Hungarian

Army, where she would come face-to-face with the perils of war and the damages of conflict, both on the body and on the mind.

In a way, she was following in the footsteps of her idol: Marie Curie had also left her laboratory for the battlefield, driving a vehicle people had dubbed the "Little Curie," upon which she carried X-ray equipment and other materials used on the front lines. Did Marie Curie reflect on the horrors of war? Did she face the moral dilemmas Lise was now pondering? There was no way of knowing, but Lise suspected that it was impossible to come face-to-face with the evil of combat and not wonder about one's role in it.

As she helped the wounded and looked at their X-rays, Lise was shocked by what she saw. The injuries were horrendous, insidious, and deadly, and more often than not, the patients died a long and painful death.

But as she considered those deaths, she also thought of Marie and Pierre Curie, whose lives had inspired her own. The Curies had worked as much as possible because they had suspected that radium existed, that it was there to be discovered. It was their scientific curiosity that had prompted them to move forward, not some grand design. The same scientific curiosity to discover had pushed Lise's own work.

That the Curies' curiosity led to X-rays was a beneficial outcome, but one they had really not intended. It had just happened. Yet radium could also kill those who inhaled it for too long.

The brutal conditions, the gruesome wounds that Lise saw, gave her a deeper understanding of human nature and of her role as a scientist in the world at large. She felt a growing obligation to ask questions she had never bothered with before: Did she have a responsibility toward her fellow human beings? Did she have to think about the repercussions of what she did before she embarked on experiments? And if so, should the answer stop her from more elaborate scientific inquiries? Things no longer seemed as clear-cut as they had during her early university days.

Now another war was being fought, and she decided she did not want to go to America and leave her family and friends in Europe, not knowing what would happen to them. She would rather take her chances in Europe, she told everyone. She wanted to remain where she was, she repeated to the British and the Americans. She did not want to have anything to do with a bomb.

Unlike Lise Meitner, Elizabeth Rona had decided to leave Europe. She felt there was no reason for her to remain in Hungary any longer than necessary. She watched as her country was threatened on both sides: to the east, there were the Russians, and to the west, the Germans. She hoped that Hungary would remain free, but there was no reason for her to stay.

Her application to go to the United States through the

Emergency Committee in Aid of Displaced Foreign Scholars had been denied. This program, which found teaching positions in American universities for teachers, scientists, and scholars persecuted by the Nazis, had seemed like the perfect way out of Europe for her. She had not been surprised by the denial, though she was deeply disappointed. Elizabeth would have to find another way to reach America.

She did receive a visitor visa, which allowed her to enter the United States for a limited period. Before leaving, she took a short detour to Vienna to visit a friend, who picked her up at the train station and drove her to the home of her former boss, Stefan Meyer. There she found old friends who had gathered to say their good-byes.

Despite the fact that her scientific skills were needed on the Manhattan Project, Elizabeth had yet to hear from any of the project's officials. She was confident that eventually something would open up that would make use of her talents. In the meantime, she walked the streets of her new city. She loved New York City, the excitement that permeated its neighborhoods and its streets. In fact, she enjoyed everything about this new country, particularly the fact that in America she didn't need to hide what little money she had behind wood paneling, as she had as a young woman.

Her favorite activity became strolling through Central Park, looking at the blooming flowers, and she often couldn't help recalling childhood days in Hungary and the early-spring days she had spent with her grandmother watching nature come to life. To the older woman's delight, Elizabeth was the grandchild who shared her fascination with nature, who did not mind observing a plant as it developed day by day and jotting down its progress in a journal, who didn't mind admiring the different shades of green as they intensified, and who didn't mind charting the growth of the pine tree her grandmother had planted as a sapling decades earlier.

As a child, Elizabeth had learned to speak French from a family that came every summer to stay near her relatives and whose three boys taught her the language. It came in handy later, as her career as a scientist blossomed. Scientists often arrived at their home to study with her father, an eminent physician. Elizabeth also had a sister, Marie, and these scientists, from all over Europe and from places as far away as Japan, had delighted the girls with tales of their countries and taught them bits of their own languages. Thus, the girls had become comfortable with people of every nationality, color, and creed.

As Elizabeth waited to find work in the United States, she mentally performed the experiments for which she had become well known while working in European laboratories—the same experiments she had performed alongside Lise in Berlin.

Some four months after arriving in New York, she attended the annual meeting of the American Physical Society, where employers looked for potential candidates. There she met a European scientist, Karl Herzfeld, who was a well-known theoretical physicist at the Catholic University of America in Washington, DC. They talked about their new lives in America, and Elizabeth Rona told him of her inability to land a job related to science. She also explained that she would need a place to work once her visa expired in order to extend her stay. Would she be interested in teaching at Trinity College in Washington, DC? he asked. He knew they were looking for a faculty instructor to teach chemistry and other science classes. Elizabeth Rona said yes.

Teaching would not be difficult for her. She had sharpened her teaching skills early in her career, at the University of Budapest, when Dr. Francis Tangl, a famous biochemist and physiologist, hired her to write and teach courses that complemented the training of his graduate students. She had found it a strange spot to be in: She was the only woman in the program, and she was younger than the students for whom she was putting together the courses.

These were medical students, and they reminded her of the wish she had held of becoming a doctor herself, a dream erased by her father's adamant opposition. Oddly enough, that teaching experience turned out better than she had anticipated. Of course, she knew that the situation would be markedly different in Washington, DC, at Trinity, but she suspected that she would thrive there as well. She always did.

While preparing to move to Washington, she often recalled her earliest days in America, not so many months before. She had known that some of her former colleagues had ended up in New York and had gone to work at Columbia University. And so it was there that she headed as soon as she landed. In the physics department at Columbia she met not only Fermi and Szilard but also several other scientists she had known intimately in Europe, and a handful she had never met before. And she thought of the earliest women researchers with whom she had crossed paths, the ones who had been her colleagues and had become her friends. They had learned from one another and traveled together to various European laboratories to study and learn.

But it seemed that things were done differently in the laboratories of the United States. At Columbia, no one spoke to her, and she didn't know what to make of that fact. She could have easily talked shop with any of these people, as by the time she landed in the United States, she had already worked with Lise and Hahn at the Kaiser Wilhelm Institute in Berlin; with Meyer at the Institute for Radium Research in Vienna; and with the Curies in Paris. But no one spoke to her, about science or anything else. Even a young scientist she had known quite well, and to whom a mutual friend had asked her to extend his hellos, simply turned away and walked off.

She didn't know it then, but there were FBI agents at Columbia. They were questioning everybody about her visit there: she, a European scientist with a visitor visa, traipsing in a laboratory where a secret project was taking place. They feared that she was a German spy sent to the United States to infiltrate the laboratories, uncover their secret operations, and report back to her superiors.

When people first saw her, they seemed struck by the picture she presented. By the time she arrived in the United States, she was a mature woman in her early fifties wearing comfortable loafers and long skirts. Her stockings, which she wore routinely even in the spring and summer, were as heavy as wool, and her hair was speckled heavily with silver. She gave the impression of a kindly grandmother on her way to buy a toy for her grandchild, which she didn't have. She was neither a wife nor a mother, much less a grandmother.

One night, while working late at Trinity College in Washington, DC, she received a telegram from Brian O'Bryen marked RESTRICTED. That word alone had been enough to spark her imagination. The telegram read in part: "In connection with a certain war work, immediate need has arisen for large quantities of polonium, and probably also for lead-210. A stockpile of radon seeds will be available. At first, it will be necessary to produce these elements in amounts corresponding to about 50 milligrams of radium, and it is desired to obtain this quantity in the shortest period of time. It is probable that considerably larger amounts will be needed thereafter. Solutions of polonium-210 and lead-210 should be without contamination with inactive material. It is also desirable that these solutions should be strong and either not at all or slightly acidic. I believe that your unusual experience in radiochemistry will ensure quick and reliable results. You would be making a substantial contribution to the war effort."

O'Bryen had become aware that Elizabeth was in the country and was teaching at Trinity College. Since she had since been cleared as a spy, her skills on plutonium could be used.

Elizabeth reread the telegram and immediately drafted a letter stating that she was interested. The following evening, while gathering her paperwork in her office, she heard a knock on the door. There stood a very tall and thin man who introduced himself as Professor Brian O'Bryen. As they sat together drinking tea, he described, as much as he could, the enormous covert operation taking place in various cities in America; he also told her that he wanted her to take part in it, if she was willing. They were building a bomb, he told her, one they planned to use to end the war with the Nazis. Elizabeth looked at a photo affixed on the wall. Her friends back in Hungary smiled back at her. Some of them, she knew, had already died.

chapter nineteen

Trinity

It was a warm morning that July 16, 1945, in the desert of New Mexico, some 120 miles south of Santa Fe. The blast had been scheduled for dawn, but a sudden passing storm had delayed the experiment for hours, and it was only as five o'clock neared that the go-ahead was given.

The test had taken many months to set up. Early that morning, those who had been involved in it—the dozens of scientists, engineers, and military and government officials, as well as individuals who had been invited to view it—had left their homes and hotels while it was still dark and had driven to the test site. They had watched the dark sky, anticipating how it would soon light up as if it were morning.

The test had required a good-size piece of wide and flat land, as they knew this would give them better fallout measurements after the explosion. They had also wanted the test site to be a good distance from the populated area of Los Alamos, away from curious eyes. The distance served another purpose: Following the explosion, the fallout on the inhabitants would not be too dangerous.

President Truman had known about the test from the start and, along with the rest, had agreed with General Groves to pick an area where no Native Americans were residing, so that they would not be displaced from their homes. The area had been a practice bombing and air-to-air gunnery range for B-29 and B-17 planes, so the nearby population was accustomed to hearing odd explosions.

In the middle of the large expanse of land, a one-hundred-foot steel tower had been erected, above which the bomb itself was secured. Scientists had developed several ways in which the bomb could have been constructed—measuring, calculating, scrawling various possibilities on paper and blackboards—and finally settled on an aerial burst as the option likely to give them the most effective results.

Some two hundred people knew of the classified operation, but only a few had been given permission to attend. Those few could not help themselves; they stared up at the bomb in astonishment, as it dawned on them that what had been only a possibility up until this point was now a tangible reality. They could hike up and touch its cool metal, if they had been allowed to, although only J. Robert Oppenheimer did that; they could sense its weight. It was a real thing. With the flick of a switch, with a slow countdown, the bomb would go off and they would blast into the unknown. It was a frightening yet very exciting thought, they would admit later on, even if only to those few who persisted in asking.

Several of the scientists who had not been invited to watch the test had, regardless of regulations, crawled onto the nearby borderland, which was made up of more than a thirty-mile radius, intent on being witnesses to history. Several scientists moved into the photo bunkers, the closest locations they could find to view the explosion. Now they found themselves ready to watch the first nuclear test explosion as it pierced the predawn air.

President Franklin Delano Roosevelt had died three months earlier, on April 12, and Vice President Harry S. Truman had taken his place, becoming the thirty-third president of the United States. While serving as vice president, Truman had not been aware of the Manhattan Project, though he had suspected that some kind of secret military operation was under way. But soon after taking office, he had been briefed on the rush to complete the atomic bomb, and he had agreed to go forward with the test. He knew what was happening in New Mexico, and he eagerly awaited word of the outcome.

Up until 1942, the possibility of building a bomb had been just that: a possibility. Despite numerous discoveries and scientific advances, no one knew for certain if it could be done. But after December 2, 1942, when Fermi and the other scientists in his University of Chicago research group, beneath the stands of Stagg Field stadium, had successfully tested sustaining a chain reaction long enough to make a bomb, the possibility had become reality.

The evening prior to the Trinity test in New Mexico, many of the people involved in it, including General Groves, were asked to stay near the bunkers at base camp, located some ten miles away. Such a precaution was especially necessary for General Groves: He and Oppenheimer, the two men in charge of the entire operation, were not to be in the same place at the same time, so that in the event that something catastrophic happened, at least one of them would still be there to give orders.

As this was the first test of a nuclear bomb, no one knew exactly what would happen. Nuclear fission had never been attempted at this scale, and some of the scientists, deep down, were afraid that the test would ignite the atmosphere and cause global destruction; while this was a very distant possibility, the extinction of the human race seemed to them to be a real option. But many others didn't believe that anything would happen at all, thinking that all their efforts would go out in a flicker of nothingness.

For days every calculation had been done and redone, checked and rechecked; every wire, knob, and pile had been secured and tied down; weather reports had been looked at and adjustments made depending on cloud patterns and wind shifts. Yet the reality was that they were trying something new, and something could always go wrong.

General Groves, the man in charge of the entire operation, had made plans for all imaginable eventualities, including evacuating nearby towns and implementing martial law if anything horrifying should occur. But he didn't want to think of that possibility. He was conscious of his image, of how he came across in the press and to his superiors. He worried about what others would say of him after the war, particularly if the bomb turned out to be a dud. "Think of me standing before a US Senate committee after the war when it asks me: 'General Groves, why did you spend *this* million or *that* million of dollars?'" he told Oppenheimer. But while he was concerned about his superiors, he didn't care all that much about the scientists. He didn't like them, nor was he bothered by what they thought of him; he always pushed them to do better and to finish on time. And he was aware that they liked him as much as he liked them.

Many of the attendees began to feel chilly, and it was on the rain that they blamed their shivers, not on the nerves they were experiencing. They tried to behave normally, as if this were just another day, another experiment that they were performing in the comfort of their laboratories. But they all knew better, and it showed on their faces, in their twitchy movements, in the muttering of their lips, in the numerous packets of cigarettes they consumed, even though they had been warned not to smoke, given all the wiring snaking around them.

Oppenheimer was pale and tense and could barely catch his breath. Those near him feared intruding on his thoughts, so they stayed some feet away and left him to his own devices. More than anybody else, he was aware of the dangers behind the bomb's science: what could happen if it didn't work, but also what would happen if it did. The pressure seemed to crush him; it was unlike anything he had ever felt before, or would ever feel again. That sense of unease grew as the countdown started. He knew that lives depended on the outcome of the test.

At supper the night before the test, the attendees had been advised about what to do during the explosion to prevent eye damage; to prevent irradiation; to prevent ear damage; to prevent being knocked down to the ground. In essence, they were advised to wear goggles; not to look directly toward the blast, if they could restrain themselves; to wear earplugs, although the sound would penetrate regardless; and to hold on to something, for even though they would be standing some distance from the blast, the ground beneath them was likely to tremble, and they might find themselves losing their balance. The blast would be the loudest, brightest thing they would ever see, they were told. They needed to take precautions. And now, with zero hour approaching, they tried to remember what they had been told.

As the time for the firing arrived, it was hard to imagine that all those weeks and months of preparation were finally coming to this. Looking up, all could see the bomb resting in its tower, appearing not particularly threatening. The surrounding area was becoming crowded, with everyone waiting to take their places when the signal was given.

Rain came down heavily, and they even noticed some rumbles of thunder; those in attendance wondered whether the test would go forward, and if it did, how the weather would influence the outcome. The 4:00 AM detonation had been canceled, and as they inched toward morning, the rain still came down with abandon. The lightning, in particular, was a big concern, as miles of wiring were attached to the bomb and sticking out from the now soaked ground. Any electrical surge could prove disastrous.

But at 5:29 AM, as city lights flickered dimly in the distance, scientists flipped a switch for the detonation and held their collective breath. They heard a brilliantly loud burst, and in that moment, all their studies, all their expertise, all their research and theory became reality. The bomb worked flawlessly and produced an explosion brighter than anyone had thought possible. A huge cloud billowed upward, reaching an elevation of nearly forty thousand feet, the light visible almost two hundred miles away. Val Fitch, a scientist who witnessed the blast, said later: "It took the blast wave about thirty seconds. There was the initial loud report, the sharp gust of wind, and then the long period of reverberation as the sound waves echoed off the nearby mountains and came back to us."

Several scientists hopped into their trucks and for some time followed the radioactive clouds that trailed above them, some wondering where they would travel to, where the fallout would eventually land, and how far it would go. Some days later, they learned that it had rained in Illinois and that the rain had brought down small amounts of radioactive fallout; the clouds had traveled some fifteen hundred miles. Immediately after the blast, Fermi and Oppenheimer had calculated that the energy yield of the test was equivalent to about 20,000 tons of TNT.

The witnesses no longer felt chilly. They sensed the heat coming toward them as the fireball grew and changed in color from yellow to orange to red, watching it climb upward toward the sky like a slithering snake. After a few minutes, it became dark again, but in the sky and over the surrounding area, there remained a purple glow few of them ever managed to forget.

Those scientists who lived in the vicinity soon jumped

into their jeeps and cars and returned home, where they quickly shed their clothing, headed into their showers, and scrubbed themselves with hot water and soap, over and over again, as if the simple act of cleansing their bodies might help them get rid of the radioactive material, should they have been contaminated. Again and again they did so, later throwing the clothes they had been wearing into dumpsters.

What had transpired in New Mexico was never supposed to happen. Although atomic science had been a subject pursued with excitement in Europe, the idea of an atomic bomb had seemed like an impossibility.

According to scientific theories of the era, the atom was made up of a nucleus that contained positively charged particles named protons and neutrally charged neutrons; a good distance from the nucleus were electrons, or negatively charged particles, equal in number to the protons. The two never met. With the discovery of the structure of the atom, talk of harnessing the energy within it became a popular subject within the scientific community, particularly in the 1930s. For many, however, this had seemed more like science fiction than reality. "Nonsense," Ernest Rutherford, one of the most famous physicists of the time, had been inspired to say. Nonsense. It was unimaginable.

But here were the intrepid Americans, this July 1945,

having successfully done the impossible: They had tested an atomic bomb. What had been debated and thought about for decades had taken them less than four years to achieve, proceeding from a somewhat abstract idea to an actual weapon the likes of which no one had ever seen. The reality of it was staggering.

The scientific community greeted the news with mixed reactions. There were those who foresaw what was to come—what in their minds meant the end of the war. However, there were also scientists who wished that the experiments had not come to fruition and that nuclear fission had remained science fiction, much as Rutherford had declared it to be. They also foresaw what was to come, but their view of the future was much darker and bleaker.

General Groves was not one who debated the moral questions, nor did he believe that scientists should place their conscience above their work. He did not believe scientists had any right to question whether the bomb should be built at all, much less how it had to be used. Their job was simply to construct it and to test it. The military had the final say, General Groves told them. Morality had no place in the military. They were fighting a war, and there was no time to ask all these philosophical questions.

General Groves was thrilled with the outcome of the Trinity test, which he saw as his dress rehearsal. It was a major step forward, and he was now eager to move ahead with the real thing. But Oppenheimer, Groves's right-hand man, was suddenly overwhelmed with fear. What had they done? What would they do now? Famously, those who stood by him heard him whisper a notorious passage from Hindu scriptures: "Now I am become Death, the destroyer of worlds."

chapter twenty

The End and the Beginning

I n September 1939, Hitler and his army invaded Poland. In June 1940, it was France's turn to fall to the Germans, and a year later, the Nazis invaded the Soviet Union. From afar, the United States watched as these events played out and crippled Europe and the Pacific. Then, on December 7, 1941, the Japanese attacked Pearl Harbor. Throwing isolation aside, the United States answered this attack with a declaration of war, and the country was finally plunged into World War II.

Aside from being the month when the United States entered the war, December 1941 held another distinction: It was at this time that the federal Office of Scientific Research and Development (OSRD) decided to delve deeply into researching plutonium, the new element scientists had isolated a year earlier at the University of California, Berkeley. The OSRD gave a contract not only to that university but also to the University of Chicago (Met Lab) to continue their studies, and from that day on, the war was fought on two fronts. On the one hand, there was the military front, which the papers reported on with huge headlines and which people followed religiously; and on the other hand, there was the scientific front, the secret scientific track that people knew very little about and that would come to life some years down the road.

In 1945, as World War II continued to rage in both Europe and the Pacific, the Manhattan Project was in full swing. But while the secret project was progressing well, the scientists were still not sure if or when the bomb would be completed, or how it would be used.

Then, two developments shocked the world: First, President Roosevelt died, making way for Truman to become president of the United States; and a few weeks later, on May 7, Nazi Germany surrendered. Having been warned by his officers that the Russians were only days away from the chancellery in Berlin, Hitler chose to die by suicide on April 30, and shortly thereafter his country gave up.

While the war in Germany was over, President Truman found himself in a terrible predicament. The July Trinity test in New Mexico had proved successful and given him an unrivaled weapon that could bring destruction to a city within seconds. Should he use it against Japan? The United

States and Japan were still locked in a terrible struggle, with tensions higher than they had ever been before; despite the fact that Japan was being relentlessly bombarded by air raids, the Japanese refused to surrender.

President Truman had two options: He could drop the atomic bomb on Japan or he could become involved in a land invasion of the country, which already had been discussed and code-named Operation Downfall. But Truman knew that such an invasion would cost thousands of American lives. It wasn't an easy choice, but records show that he was looking for a way to end the war quickly and with as little loss of life on the American side as possible. The outcome was to change not only the course of the war but of history forever.

On July 26, the United States, the United Kingdom, and China issued a warning, with President Truman broadcasting an ultimatum on the air: "We call upon the government of Japan to proclaim now the unconditional surrender of all Japanese armed forces, and to provide proper and adequate assurances of their good faith in such action. The alternative for Japan is prompt and utter destruction."

The island of Tinian was chosen as the base of operations for the atomic bomb attack against Japan. However, there was not going to be any direct connection between Tinian and Los Alamos, where the bomb had been built. Everything had to go through Washington. Oppenheimer did not like that. Having overseen every detail of the bomb's construction, he wanted to be in close touch with Tinian and with the plane that was going to drop the bomb. There were many ways in which this could go wrong, and he had prepared for such possibilities. Having to go through Washington was an extra step that he didn't need, one that would waste time in case of an emergency.

Colonel Paul Tibbets was at the helm of the *Enola Gay*, the plane that was to drop the bomb. Colonel Tibbets was a very experienced pilot, whose previous missions had taken him to Europe and North Africa. Upon his return to the United States, he started working as an engineer for B-29 planes, as well as test-piloting them. He had learned that he would become involved in the Manhattan Project from his father when he received a strange telephone call from Tibbets Sr. telling him that military officers had been snooping around their hometown of Miami, asking about him. Some days later, Uzal Ent, commander of the Second Air Force, had called him, inviting him to meet right away in his office in Colorado Springs, Colorado.

On arriving in Colorado Springs, Colonel Tibbets met and spoke with two additional men besides Uzal Ent, Captain William S. Parsons and Dr. Norman F. Ramsey Jr., whereupon he was told that he had been selected for a special mission. This was a confidential mission, they emphasized, as he sat in the office, listening as Dr. Ramsey, a professor of physics, explained the makings of the atomic bomb.

He was not to say anything about the Manhattan Project, the bomb, or his mission, but he would be allowed to choose the site where he would train, and he could pick his crew. Realizing that the men were serious and unwilling to answer any further questions, Colonel Tibbets agreed to go along and selected Wendover, Utah, as a training site, as well as a few men he already knew as his crew.

At about two o'clock in the morning (noon in Washington) on Sunday, August 6, 1945, the *Enola Gay* left the small Pacific island of Tinian. "It was a pleasant tropical night," Colonel Tibbets later wrote. "Around us were cream-puff clouds, their edges outlined by the faint glow of a crescent moon." The flight was uneventful, and Tibbets and the rest of the crew enjoyed watching a striking sunrise. "And now we were winging toward Japan," Colonel Tibbets recalled, "surrounded by scattered clouds that were edged with reddish gold from the slanting light of the newly risen sun."

Not ten minutes before they were to drop the bomb, Hiroshima appeared, as early-morning sunlight "glistened off the white buildings in the distance." The city, aside from its nearly 300,000 inhabitants, was also home to an army base, with 43,000 soldiers.

Thomas Ferebee, the bombardier, caught a glimpse of the Aioi Bridge, the target where he was supposed to drop the bomb. The crew's navigator, Theodore Van Kirk, also saw the bridge as he glanced out the window. It was 8:15 AM when the bomb dropped over Hiroshima. With the plane now so much lighter, Colonel Tibbets hurried to get as far as possible from the scene.

Once they knew the effects of the bomb could not interfere with the plane's flight path, Colonel Tibbets brought the plane close enough so that they could catch a glimpse of the damage. But they were not ready for what they saw. It was as if they were witnessing a living thing beneath them, moving and slithering upward. "The city we had seen so clearly in the sunlight a few minutes before was now an ugly smudge," said Colonel Tibbets.

To Theodore Van Kirk, it appeared like "a pot of boiling black oil."

And suddenly, the reality of what had just happened swept over them. "My God, what have we done?" whispered Robert Lewis, the copilot.

Tinian and Washington were scheduled to be in continuous communication, but the island was silent for the entire afternoon, with the officials in Washington unaware of what was happening. They heard nothing at noon, as had been planned. As it turned out, the takeoff report didn't come to Washington until later that evening. Settled in General Groves's office, officials were pacing up and down, trying to quiet their nerves.

The report arrived late, at precisely the time when they should have been receiving news of what the strike had done to the city of Hiroshima. They read the paper and waited for more news, but none came. Where was the plane now? Finally, at around eleven thirty that evening, they received another report from the plane.

"Clear cut, successful in all respects," read Colonel Tibbets's report. "Visual effects greater than Alamogordo [the Trinity test site]." He also let them know that he was back at base camp. While those on the plane would always remember what they had witnessed and live with the sense of dread at what the bomb over Hiroshima had done, for those in Washington there was only a great sense of accomplishment and a shout of exhilaration at the bomb's success. They had done it.

General Groves called Oppenheimer in Los Alamos to let him know that the bomb had exploded over Hiroshima, that it had worked better than the one at Trinity, and that he was proud of him and of everyone at Los Alamos. General Groves congratulated everyone on a job well done.

The scientists at Los Alamos, and by extension everyone who had been involved in the Manhattan Project, learned about the bomb over Hiroshima after the mission was completed. While Lise Meitner had refused to participate in its development and never wanted to travel to Los Alamos, her nephew, Otto Robert Frisch, had agreed to do a bit of work for the Americans and found himself in Los Alamos when Hiroshima was destroyed. He heard the thunderous running of his colleagues as they rushed down the corridors, shouting to one another that the bomb had exploded, that the Japanese city had been obliterated.

Otto Robert Frisch suddenly recalled the discovery of fission a handful of years earlier, during that Christmas holiday he had spent talking science with his aunt. Some calculations and a sudden moment of inspiration had evolved into this historic moment. He was frightened by what Lise's reaction would be upon learning what had just occurred in Japan. He would never tell her how many of his colleagues had laughed and congratulated one another on a job well done; how the death of possibly hundreds of thousands of people had prompted many of them to toast one another, or to reserve tables in the city's better-known restaurants in order to celebrate their success. While he understood that they felt rewarded for having completed a job others had only imagined, he thought some of their reactions "ghoulish." No, Frisch would never tell any of that to his aunt, Lise.

But he would tell her about those who felt as she did, those who wished the bomb had never come to fruition. About the ones whose sudden desire to flee the Tech Area had overwhelmed them, and how as he left the area he could not help noticing a few of his colleagues vomiting in the bushes or rushing to the bathrooms for a bit of privacy.

President Truman made his announcement about the bomb's explosion at eleven o'clock the next morning, telling the American people about the detonation over Hiroshima. The world was listening, too.

However, Japan had not yet surrendered. The Americans wanted Japan to surrender unconditionally, but the country was still hanging on. A second bomb then hit the city of Nagasaki. Japan surrendered on August 15, 1945; Emperor Hirohito refused to allow more death to come to his people. The war was over.

The twin blasts killed more than two hundred thousand people in the immediate aftermath, and the world learned of the devastating effects that atomic weapons could have. These attacks marked the first time that such catastrophic bombs were used, though the aftereffects have lasted for decades.

Despite the women's contributions, it was the men who gained the prestige and opportunities coming out of the Manhattan Project. *Life* magazine ran a series of articles on the project, and the writer profiled those he believed had made the greatest contributions to the bombs: Enrico Fermi, of course; J. Robert Oppenheimer; Edward Teller; and General Leslie Groves. These men, the writer said, had worn the "tunic of Superman." Readers wanted to know everything about them. Who were they, and where had they come from? How did they work, and where did they find their inspiration? Did they take sugar in their coffee? Did they prefer lemon or milk in their tea? Were they married?

Although Lise Meitner had explained nuclear fission, and with that explanation changed the way scientists looked at atomic science, in essence opening the door to the atomic bomb, she was hardly acknowledged for her contributions, least of all by Hahn, who went on to earn a Nobel Prize for the discovery, having worked alongside the other member of their Berlin team, Fritz Strassmann.

The science historian Ruth Lewin Sime said this about Hahn's behavior toward Lise Meitner: "Had Hahn made an effort to set the scientific record straight, had he spoken of their long friendship and collaboration, of her leadership of the Berlin team or her contributions to the fission discovery, it would have helped. But he did not. In his mind the discovery had become his, and his alone. In his many interviews he never spoke of his work with Meitner; not once did he even mention her name.... Meitner and her friends were appalled."

Others bestowed upon Lise Meitner the credit that Otto Hahn did not give her. In November 1945, the *Atlantic Monthly* quoted Albert Einstein as saying: "I do not consider myself the father of the release of atomic energy. My part in it was quite indirect. I did not, in fact, foresee that it would be released in my time. I believed only that it was theoretically possible....It was discovered by Hahn in Berlin, and he himself misinterpreted what he discovered. It was Lise Meitner who provided the correct interpretation."

On July 16, 1945, when the first atomic bomb was tested in New Mexico and its loud booms pierced the early-dawn sky, it was hailed as the ushering in of the atomic era. Photographs taken for posterity's sake show the New Mexico desert prior to the explosion and immediately thereafter; the process of building the bomb and the many miles of wires stretching across its pathways; the forklift lifting the bomb into position. Among the hundreds of photos, there are also those revealing the faces of the scientists, technicians, and officials who worked toward that moment: Oppenheimer, smiling but looking tired; General Groves, surveying the area prior to the detonation and in the hours afterward; Fermi and his colleagues in wrinkly business suits holding tight but obviously satisfied grins, for the results of their experiments were precisely what they had expected; and young army men, wet from the recent downpours, standing alongside the officials.

But anyone who views those photographs will become aware of a strange fact: Very few of the snapshots feature a woman.

In the articles that appeared immediately after the test

in July 1945, and in the stories, books, and personal biographies that were published after the bombing of Hiroshima and Nagasaki in August 1945, there was hardly any mention of the top-notch female scientists who helped with the development of the nuclear bomb, despite the fact that they had been there, overseeing the project from near and far, contributing to such a degree, one could safely say, that without their knowledge the men who worked on the bomb would not have been able to achieve their goals.

How the female scientists reacted to the outcome of their contributions to the bomb depended on their personal views of science and on their beliefs about how such discoveries could help or hurt humanity. In the wake of the detonations, many were proud of their contributions, for they had helped to end World War II. But others expressed concerns and were stunned by what had occurred, by the number of people who had died, and by how many were still suffering and would continue to suffer. They had been aware that there would be consequences, but as Laura Fermi wrote later in her book: "A blow is no less painful for being expected."

Whatever their feelings, no one can deny, least of all themselves, that these female scientists were leaders in their fields and that they had a hand in one of the most powerful events that has shaped the course of history.

PHOTOGRAPHS

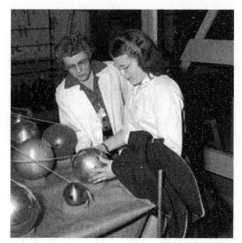

Elizabeth "Diz" Graves (left, with her daughter, right) was a pioneering physicist who worked at the Los Alamos National Laboratory in New Mexico during World War II. She became one of the highest-ranking women of the Manhattan Project.

Hungarian nuclear chemist Elizabeth Rona is best known for her work in radioactive isotopes. She developed an enhanced method for preparing polonium samples, and her techniques were highly coveted by the Manhattan Project scientists.

Marie Curie (right) was a Polish-born French chemist and physicist who became the first person and only woman to win two Nobel Prizes. Her daughter, Irène Joliot-Curie (left), followed in her mother's footsteps, also winning a Nobel Prize in Chemistry, in 1935.

German-American theoretical physicist Maria Goeppert-Mayer (right, with her husband, Joseph, left) became the second woman to win the Nobel Prize in Physics, after Marie Curie.

Lise Meitner (right) was an Austrian physicist known for her work in radioactivity and nuclear physics. Otto Hahn (left) was her partner for many years in Berlin, until he betrayed her in 1944 when he received the Nobel Prize in Chemistry for the discovery of nuclear fission and didn't credit her.

Renowned American scientist Leona Woods (back center) is known for helping build the first nuclear reactor and atomic bomb. She was both the youngest person and only woman to help build Chicago Pile-1.

Italian-American physicist Enrico Fermi created the first official nuclear reactor, Chicago Pile-1, beneath the stands of Stagg Field in Chicago, and led the Los Alamos team that developed the nuclear bombs.

A testing facility in the desert of New Mexico, Los Alamos had originally been built during World War II by the United States government exclusively to build nuclear weapons.

General Leslie Groves (right) directed the Manhattan Project, and J. Robert Oppenheimer (left), also known as "the father of the atomic bomb," was the head of the Los Alamos laboratory.

Oppenheimer chose to name the test Trinity after a poem by the English poet John Donne. The site was known as Jornada del Muerto, or Journey of Death. It was located about 210 miles from Los Alamos.

On Monday, July 16, 1945, the detonation of Trinity gave birth to the atomic age. Moments after the explosion, those present saw a huge mushroom cloud rise in the desert toward the sky.

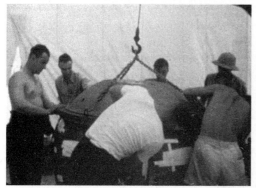

Given that such an experiment had never been performed before, every detail of the atomic bomb had to be meticulously checked and rechecked. Oppenheimer had to make certain it was ready for detonation.

On August 6, 1945, crew members on the *Enola Gay* plane dropped the first nuclear bomb, on the Japanese city of Hiroshima. The crew included Colonel Paul Tibbets, Jr., Captain Robert Lewis, Major Thomas Ferebee, Captain Theodore Van Kirk, and Captain William S. Parsons.

This infamous photograph, taken by tail gunner Bob Caron from the *Enola Gay*, shows the mushroom cloud that formed shortly after the United States dropped the first atomic bomb, over Hiroshima.

PHOTOGRAPHS

The bomb leveled most of the city and claimed about 140,000 lives. Prior to this, Hiroshima had been one of Japan's most industrialized cities.

On the morning of August 9, 1945, the United States dropped the second atomic bomb on Japan, this time on the city of Nagasaki. It is estimated that between 39,000 and 80,000 people died, with half of those deaths occurring on the first day of the attack.

AUTHOR'S NOTE

I became obsessed with the work of the female scientists involved with the Manhattan Project when I read a short article on Elizabeth Rona. While I knew a lot about the project already, having read several books on the subject, it surprised me that I had never come across her name. As I dug deeper, I realized that she was not the only case of omission: There were many female scientists whose contributions played a key role in the success of the mission but who had somehow fallen to the wayside. Their involvement was not noted in most history books, which mainly focused on the well-known male scientists. I found it odd, sad, and disappointing that these women had been erased from history. Why was their work on the project neglected? Who were these women scientists? Where did they come from, and why did they decide to work on the Manhattan Project? I wanted to know what inspired them to be involved. While I could not include every woman on the project, I knew I had to share some of their stories.

During my research, I learned about the morality of science and the difference between what can and should be done. Many of these women were not fully aware of the consequences of such a powerful weapon, and when the amount of destruction came to light, they struggled with their involvement. It begged the question: Can scientists do their job and still maintain a sense of moral responsibility?

I hope that readers will use this text as a springboard to learn more about the women who have made important contributions to science throughout history. The aspirations, frustrations, and desires women felt back in the 1940s are still very relevant today. While we have made great strides as a society to give women the attention they deserve in the sciences, there is still a lot of work to be done. But I hope that the stories of these atomic women leave readers feeling hopeful for the future—especially the future of science.

ACKNOWLEDGMENTS

I'd like to thank the Emilio Segrè Visual Archives; the American Institute of Physics; Mary Straka, science librarian at the Argonne Research Library, Argonne National Laboratory; the Smithsonian Institution Archives; Allison Rein, at the Niels Bohr Library & Archives; Alexandra Levy, at the Atomic Heritage Foundation; the Los Alamos Historical Archives; and Brown University Department of Mathematics. At Little, Brown Books for Young Readers, my wonderful editors Alvina Ling and Samantha Gentry, and the entire staff. And, as always, my thanks go to the wonderfully talented Rob Weisbach, agent and friend extraordinaire. Gratitude to my mother, Celeste, and my sister, Francesca, for listening to me rattle on about atomic energy and female scientists and the joys of writing.

SCIENTIFIC TIMELINE

— 1896 —

Henri Becquerel, a French scientist, publishes his research on penetrating radioactivity, which he noticed was being emitted by uranium compounds.

Marie Curie is tantalized by this discovery and vows to tackle Becquerel's research.

— 1898 —

Marie Curie adds to Henri Becquerel's research by discovering that the elements thorium and uranium emit similar radiation. She also discovers polonium and radium.

— 1905 —

Albert Einstein publishes papers explaining his theory of special relativity.

— 1911 —

Ernest Rutherford discovers the nucleus in the atom.

— 1932 —

The English physicist James Chadwick tells the world about his discovery of the neutron, which spurs further experiments into the atom's makeup.

— 1934 —

Irène Joliot-Curie and Frédéric Joliot-Curie show that radioactivity can be achieved artificially.

In Rome, Enrico Fermi bombards uranium and other materials with neutrons but does not recognize some of his results as possible signs of nuclear fission.

— 1938 —

In December, while in Berlin, Otto Hahn and Fritz Strassmann experiment with neutron bombardment of uranium. In Sweden, their partner Lise Meitner and her nephew, Otto Frisch, work on Hahn and Strassmann's experiment and interpret the results as the splitting of the nuclei cleanly in two. They name this new phenomenon "nuclear fission."

— 1939 —

Niels Bohr attends the fifth Washington Conference on Theoretical Physics, where he speaks about nuclear fission. Scientists there are perplexed, wondering how they could have missed it, yet are inspired to use the process further, particularly for military purposes.

Enrico Fermi, who had arrived in the United States only two weeks before the conference, also attends. Niels Bohr's words intrigue Fermi, who begins to wonder about the possibility of using nuclear fission for military weaponry.

— 1939 —

By March, scientists, including the Joliot-Curies in Paris and Enrico Fermi in New York, are performing small experiments to show that nuclear fission is not only possible but that, by extension, so is a nuclear chain reaction.

By August, well-known scientists such as Leo Szilard push Albert Einstein to sign a letter to President Roosevelt, warning him that building a superbomb has now become a possibility and that the chances the Germans might already be researching and working on such a weapon are good. Scientists feel that the United States should begin its own testing.

By October, President Roosevelt, heeding the advice of the scientists, forms the Advisory Committee on Uranium, which by November is looking to begin research into nuclear fission.

The year closes with the Joliot-Curies demonstrating that the breakup of nuclei can cause a chain reaction.

— 1940 —

By March, scientists discover that fission is easier to achieve with U-235, a rare isotope, but U-238 is much more available.

By June, studies in the separation of uranium isotopes begin at Columbia University, in New York.

— 1941 —

In June, Germany, led by Adolf Hitler, invades the Soviet Union. The United States still remains out of the conflict.

By November, scientists across the United States have come to agree that building an atomic bomb is a real possibility.

The year ends with President Roosevelt committing $400,000 for research into isotope separation. This sum will jump up considerably when more people are recruited and more research gets under way.

On December 7, Japan bombs Pearl Harbor, causing the United States to enter World War II. Germany and Italy declare war on the United States.

— 1942 —

In January, Arthur Compton is hired to lead the Metallurgical Laboratory (Met Lab) at the University of Chicago, where prominent scientists begin to gather. Many who were working at Columbia University in New York move to the Chicago Met Lab.

In April, Enrico Fermi leaves Columbia University and joins the Metallurgical Laboratory in Chicago. Nathalie Goldowski and Leona Woods will eventually join him.

In June, the price of building the atomic bomb has jumped to nearly $100 million, and scientists calculate that a bomb could be ready by 1944.

By August, the building of the atomic bomb is officially under the direction of the Manhattan District of the US Army Corps of Engineers, and officially becomes known as the Manhattan Project.

In September, Colonel (later General) Leslie Groves is put in charge of the Manhattan Project.

By November, all the sites involved in the construction of the bomb have been chosen. They include Oak Ridge, Tennessee; Hanford, Washington; and Los Alamos, New Mexico.

The year ends with Enrico Fermi and his team, including Leona Woods, achieving the first self-sustaining chain reaction beneath the stands of Stagg Field at the University of Chicago.

— 1943 —

By March, J. Robert Oppenheimer has transferred to the laboratory in Los Alamos, where other scientists have also arrived.

In June, the first plutonium manufactured in a plant in Hanford, Washington, arrives in Los Alamos.

— 1944 —

By the start of the year, scientists have concluded that they will produce enough plutonium to build two bombs, not one, as everyone had predicted.

The start of the year also brings the decision by General Leslie Groves and J. Robert Oppenheimer to test a bomb. While they had initially not planned on such a test, they now agree that testing will be essential.

By August, General Leslie Groves is told that a uranium bomb will likely be ready within a year.

By October, the site for the first atomic bomb test has been chosen: the Alamogordo Bombing Range in the desert of New Mexico. General Leslie Groves approves this choice.

— 1945 —

War continues, and in February, American forces land on the Japanese island of Iwo Jima.

By April, Los Alamos has nearly fifty pounds of U-235 at its disposal. Testing of the bomb is expected in a few months, and detonation of the official bombs is planned for shortly after the test.

On April 12, President Roosevelt dies, and the new president, Harry S. Truman, is briefed on the Manhattan Project.

In May, Germany surrenders, following the suicide of Adolf Hitler.

By early July, scientists are busy preparing the bomb for the first test. Code-named Trinity, it goes off on July 16 near Alamogordo, New Mexico. Bad weather delays the detonation until dawn, but then the test takes place without a hitch and the bomb performs better than most of the scientists expected.

In July, General Leslie Groves authorizes the use of atomic bombs on enemies when such bombs become available.

On August 6, the United States drops the first-ever uranium bomb on the Japanese city of Hiroshima. President Truman goes on the air to inform the American people. The world is stunned, but Japan refuses to surrender.

Three days later, on August 9, a plutonium bomb is deployed on the city of Nagasaki.

On August 15, Japan surrenders.

On September 2, 1945, the surrender documents are signed, and World War II is officially over.

SOURCE NOTES

PROLOGUE

Descriptions of Elizabeth and Al Graves's experience in Harry Miller's Tourist Court cabin and their feelings on making the bomb, on Joan Hinton and her wanting to view the explosion, and on Elizabeth Rona's experience can be found in the following sources:

McKibbon, Dorothy. "109 East Palace." In *Standing By and Making Do: Women of Wartime Los Alamos*. Edited by Jane S. Wilson and Charlotte Serber. Los Alamos, NM: Los Alamos Historical Society, 1988.

Rona, Elizabeth. *How It Came About: Radioactivity, Nuclear Physics, Atomic Energy*. Oak Ridge, TN: Oak Ridge Associated Universities, 1978.

Ulam, S. M. *Adventures of a Mathematician*. New York: Charles Scribner's Sons, 1976.

Chapter One: ALL THAT GLITTERS

There are several wonderful biographies of Marie Curie and Pierre Curie, some translated from the French. Many include material on her life as a girl in Poland, Pierre and Marie's meeting, and her discovery of radium and polonium. If still curious, look no further than the following:

Bernal, J. D. *Science in History*. New York: Cameron Associates, 1954.

Curie, Ève. *Madame Curie*. Translated by Vincent Sheean. New York: Doubleday, Doran, 1937.

Emling, Shelley. *Marie Curie and Her Daughters: The Private Lives of Science's First Family*. New York: St. Martin's, 2012.

Giroud, Françoise. *Marie Curie: A Life*. Translated by Lydia
  Davis. New York: Holmes and Meier, 1986.
Goldsmith, Barbara. *Obsessive Genius: The Inner World of Marie
  Curie*. New York: W. W. Norton, 2005.

Chapter Two: A SHY AND QUIET GIRL

Additional depictions of Lise Meitner's childhood in Vienna and
her start in the sciences can be found in the following:

Crawford, Deborah. *Lise Meitner, Atomic Pioneer*. New York:
  Crown, 1969.
Rayner-Canham, M. F., and G. W. Rayner-Canham. "Pioneer
  Women in Nuclear Science." *American Journal of Physics* 58
  (1990): 1036–43.
Rife, Patricia. *Lise Meitner and the Dawn of the Nuclear Age*.
  Boston: Birkhäuser, 1999.
Sime, Ruth Lewin. "Lise Meitner and the Discovery of Fission."
  Journal of Chemical Education 66 (1989): 373–75.
Watkins, Sallie A. "Lise Meitner (1878–1968)." In *Women in
  Chemistry and Physics: A Biobibliographic Sourcebook*. Edited
  by Louise S. Grinstein, Rose K. Rose, and Miriam H.
  Rafailovich. Westport, CT: Greenwood Press, 1993.
Weeks, Mary Elvira. *Discovery of the Elements*. 6th ed. Easton,
  PA: Journal of Chemical Education, 1956.

Chapter Three: A LIFE IN LEARNING

For additional information on Elizabeth Rona's childhood, her
upbringing, her love of family and medicine, her meeting with Otto
Hahn, and her study with Marie Curie and Irène Joliot-Curie,
please consult the following:

Parkinson, Claire L. *Breakthroughs: A Chronology of Great
  Achievements in Science and Mathematics, 1200–1930*.
  London: Mansell, 1985.

Rona, Elizabeth. *How It Came About: Radioactivity, Nuclear
Physics, Atomic Energy.* Oak Ridge, TN: Oak Ridge
Associated Universities, 1978.
Taton, René, ed. *History of Science: Science in the Twentieth Century.*
Translated by A. J. Pomerans. New York: Basic Books, 1966.

Chapter Four: POWER COUPLE

On the lives of Irène and Frédéric Joliot-Curie, their intimate
relationship, and their relationship with Marie Curie, the following
works will give readers a deeper look:

Barr, E. Scott. "The Incredible Marie Curie and Her Family."
Physics Teacher 2 (1964): 251–59.
Bigland, Eileen. *Madame Curie.* New York: Criterion, 1957.
Curie, Ève. *Marie Curie.* Translated by Vincent Sheean. New
York: Doubleday, Doran, 1937.
Emling, Shelley. *Marie Curie and Her Daughters: The Private Lives
of Science's First Family.* New York: St. Martin's, 2012.
Goldsmith, Barbara. *Obsessive Genius: The Inner World of Marie
Curie.* New York: W. W. Norton, 2005.
Opfell, Olga. "Triumph and Rebuff: Irène Joliot-Curie." In *The
Lady Laureates: Women Who Have Won the Nobel Prize.* 2nd
ed., 165–82. Metuchen, NJ: Scarecrow Press, 1986.

Chapter Five: IN EXILE

Some texts describing Lise Meitner's discovery of nuclear fission
are better than others. The ones below detail not only her scientific
contribution to the field but also her life in exile in Sweden; her
relationship with Otto Hahn and her Berlin group; her relationship
with her nephew, Otto Frisch, which she valued; and how she felt
upon realizing what her monumental discovery would mean for the
scientific world at large.

Crawford, Deborah. *Lise Meitner, Atomic Pioneer.* New York:
Crown, 1969.

Frisch, Otto. Oral history interview by Thomas S. Kuhn, May 3, 1967, transcript. American Institute of Physics, Niels Bohr Library and Archives. http://www.aip.org /history-programs/niels-bohr-library/oral-histories/4616.

———. *What Little I Remember*. Cambridge, UK: Cambridge University Press, 1979.

Frisch, O. R. "Lise Meitner, 1878–1968." *Biographical Memoirs of the Fellows of the Royal Society* 16 (1970): 405–20.

Hahn, Otto. *Otto Hahn: A Scientific Autobiography*. New York: Charles Scribner's Sons, 1966.

Sime, Ruth Lewin. "Lise Meitner and the Discovery of Fission." *Journal of Chemical Education* 66 (1989): 373–75.

———. "Lise Meitner in Sweden 1938–1969: Exile from Physics." *American Journal of Physics* 62 (1994): 695–701.

———. *Lise Meitner: A Life in Physics*. Berkeley: University of California Press, 1996.

Taton, René, ed. *History of Science: Science in the Twentieth Century*. Translated by A. J. Pomerans. New York: Basic Books, 1966.

Watkins, Sallie A. "Lise Meitner (1878–1968)." In *Women in Chemistry and Physics: A Biobibliographic Sourcebook*. Edited by Louise S. Grinstein, Rose K. Rose, and Miriam H. Rafailovich. Westport, CT: Greenwood Press, 1993.

Weeks, Mary Elvira. *Discovery of the Elements*. 6th ed. Easton, PA: Journal of Chemical Education, 1956.

Chapter Six: A SECRET PROJECT

A number of adult books cover Otto Frisch's reaction to his aunt's discovery, Enrico Fermi's reaction and future plans to use fission, and the use of uranium, as well as the kernel of the idea for the Manhattan Project. Here is a brief list of helpful works I consulted:

Compton, Arthur Holly. *Atomic Quest*. New York: Oxford University Press, 1956.

Frisch, Otto. *What Little I Remember*. Cambridge, UK: Cambridge University Press, 1979.

Groueff, Stephane. *Manhattan Project: The Untold Story of the Making of the Atomic Bomb.* Boston: Little, Brown, 1967.

Groves, Leslie R. *Now It Can Be Told: The Story of the Manhattan Project.* New York: Harper, 1962.

Lanouette, William. *Genius in the Shadows: A Biography of Leo Szilard, the Man Behind the Bomb.* New York: Skyhorse Publishing, 2013.

Segrè, Gino, and Bettina Hoerlin. *The Pope of Physics: Enrico Fermi and the Birth of the Atomic Age.* New York: Henry Holt, 2016.

Toomey, Elizabeth. *The Manhattan Project at Hanford Site.* Images of America. Charleston, SC: Arcadia Publishing, 2015.

Truslow, Edith C. *Manhattan District History: Nonscientific Aspects of Los Alamos Project Y 1942 through 1946.* Edited by Kasha V. Thayer. Los Alamos, NM: Los Alamos Historical Society, 1991.

Wilson, Jane, ed. *All in Our Time: The Reminiscences of Twelve Nuclear Pioneers.* Chicago: Bulletin of the Atomic Scientists, 1975.

Chapter Seven: TWO OF A KIND

To learn more about the pioneering scientist Maria Goeppert-Mayer, her life in Germany, her meeting Joseph Mayer, and her work in the United States, please look up the following:

Dash, Joan. *A Life of One's Own: Three Gifted Women and the Men They Married.* New York: Harper & Row, 1973.

Ferry, Joseph P. *Maria Goeppert Mayer: Physicist.* Women in Science. Langhorne, PA: Chelsea House, 2003.

Gosling, F. G. *The Manhattan Project: Science in the Second World War.* Energy History Series. Washington, DC: US Department of Energy, 1990.

Hoddeson, Lillian, Paul W. Henriksen, Roger A. Meade, Catherine Westfall, Gordon Baym, Richard Hewlett, Alison Kerr, Robert Penneman, Leslie Redman, and Robert Seidel. *Critical Assembly: A Technical History of Los Alamos During*

the Oppenheimer Years, 1943–1945. New York: Cambridge
University Press, 1993.

Howes, Ruth H., and Caroline L. Herzenberg. "Women of the
Manhattan Project." *Technology Review* 96, no. 8 (1993):
32–40.

Rempel, Trudy D. "Maria Gertrude Goeppert Mayer (1906–
1972)." In *Women in Chemistry and Physics: A Biobibliographic
Sourcebook.* Edited by Louise S. Grinstein, Rose K. Rose, and
Miriam H. Rafailovich. Westport, CT: Greenwood Press, 1993.

Sachs, Robert G. "Maria Goeppert Mayer." In *Biographical
Memoirs* 50, 310–28. National Academy of Sciences.
Washington, DC: National Academies Press, 1979.

Chapter Eight: THE GENERAL AND THE SCIENTIST

Much has been written about General Leslie Groves's involvement
with the Manhattan Project. Much has also been made of his
relationship with J. Robert Oppenheimer. Some helpful information
can be found in these texts:

Compton, Arthur Holly. *Atomic Quest.* New York: Oxford
University Press, 1956.

Graf, William L. *Plutonium and the Rio Grande: Environmental
Change and Contamination in the Nuclear Age.* New York:
Oxford University Press, 1994.

Greenbaum, Leonard. *A Special Interest: The Atomic Energy
Commission, Argonne National Laboratory, and the Midwestern
Universities.* Ann Arbor: University of Michigan Press, 1971.

Groves, Leslie R. *Now It Can Be Told: The Story of the Manhattan
Project.* New York: Harper, 1962.

Hawkins, David. *Manhattan District History Project Y, the Los
Alamos Project.* Vol. 1, *Inception Until August 1946.* Los
Alamos, NM: Los Alamos Scientific Laboratory of the
University of California, 1961.

Kelly, Cynthia C., ed. *Manhattan Project: The Birth of the Atomic Bomb in the Words of Its Creators, Eyewitnesses, and Historians.* New York: Black Dog & Leventhal, 2009.

Lawren, William. *The General and the Bomb: A Biography of Leslie R. Groves, Director of the Manhattan Project.* New York: Dodd Mead, 1988.

Nichols, K. D. *The Road to Trinity.* New York: William Morrow, 1987.

Oak Ridge National Laboratory Review 25, nos. 3 and 4. Oak Ridge, TN: Oak Ridge National Laboratory, 1992.

Sanger, S. L., and Robert W. Mull. *Hanford and the Bomb: An Oral History of World War II.* Seattle: Living History Press, 1990.

Chapter Nine: AMERICAN LIFE

On the Mayers' home life in America, Maria Mayer's work in Baltimore, and her eventual work for the Manhattan Project, please refer to the following:

Bailey, Martha J. *American Women in Science: A Biographical Dictionary.* Denver: ABC-CLIO, 1998.

Dash, Joan. *A Life of One's Own: Three Gifted Women and the Men They Married.* New York: Harper & Row, 1973.

Ferry, Joseph P. *Maria Goeppert Mayer: Physicist.* Women in Science. Langhorne, PA: Chelsea House, 2003.

Howes, Ruth H., and Caroline L. Herzenberg. "Women in Weapons Development: The Manhattan Project." In *Women and the Use of Military Force.* Edited by Ruth H. Howes and Michael R. Stevenson. Boulder, CO: Lynne Rienner, 1993.

Kelly, Cynthia C. *Manhattan Project: The Birth of the Atomic Bomb in the Words of Its Creators, Eyewitnesses, and Historians.* New York: Black Dog & Leventhal, 2009.

McNulty, William. "World's Most Famed Scientists, En Route to Los Alamos Project, Go Through Ancient City Office." *Santa Fe New Mexican,* May 10, 1946.

Rayner-Canham, M. F., and G. W. Rayner-Canham. "Pioneer Women in Nuclear Science." *American Journal of Physics* 58 (1990): 1036–43.

Sachs, Robert G. "Maria Goeppert Mayer." In *Biographical Memoirs* 50, 310–28. National Academy of Sciences. Washington, DC: National Academies Press, 1979.

Taton, René, ed. *History of Science: Science in the Twentieth Century.* Translated by A. J. Pomerans. New York: Basic Books, 1964.

Wilson, Jane, ed. *All in Our Time: The Reminiscences of Twelve Nuclear Pioneers.* Chicago: Bulletin of the Atomic Scientists, 1975.

Chapter Ten: RECRUITING

On Joan Hinton's involvement in the Manhattan Project, please consult some of the following:

Bailey, Martha J. *American Women in Science: A Biographical Dictionary.* Denver: ABC-CLIO, 1998.

Gibson, Toni Michnovicz, and Jon Michnovicz. *Los Alamos: 1944–1947.* Images of America. Charleston, SC: Arcadia Publishing, 2005.

Los Alamos Scientific Laboratory. *Los Alamos: Beginning of an Era, 1943–1945.* Los Alamos, NM: Los Alamos Scientific Laboratory, 2008.

Manley, Kathleen E. B. "Women of Los Alamos During World War II: Some of Their Views." *New Mexico Historical Review* 65, no. 2 (1990): 252–66.

McKibbon, Dorothy. "109 East Palace." In *Standing By and Making Do: Women of Wartime Los Alamos.* Edited by Jane Wilson and Charlotte Serber. Los Alamos, NM: Los Alamos Historical Society, 1988.

McNulty, William. "World's Most Famed Scientists, En Route to Los Alamos Project, Go Through Ancient City Office." *Santa Fe New Mexican,* May 10, 1946.

Shroyer, Jo Ann. *Secret Mesa: Inside Los Alamos National Laboratory*. New York: Wiley, 1997.

Ulam, S. M. *Adventures of a Mathematician*. New York: Charles Scribner's Sons, 1976.

Wilson, Jane S., and Charlotte Serber, eds. *Standing By and Making Do: Women of Wartime Los Alamos*. Los Alamos, NM: Los Alamos Historical Society, 1988.

Chapter Eleven: LEONA

For additional information on Leona Woods, her meeting with John Marshall, and her meeting with Enrico Fermi and involvement with the Chicago Met Lab, please read the following:

Compton, Arthur Holly. *Atomic Quest*. New York: Oxford University Press, 1956.

Fermi, Laura. *Atoms in the Family: My Life with Enrico Fermi*. Chicago: University of Chicago Press, 1954.

Folkart, Burt A. "Leona Marshall Libby Dies; Sole Woman to Work on Fermi's 1st Nuclear Reactor." *Los Angeles Times*, November 13, 1986.

Libby, Leona Marshall. *The Uranium People*. New York: Crane, Russak, 1979.

Segrè, Gino, and Bettina Hoerlin. *The Pope of Physics: Enrico Fermi and the Birth of the Atomic Age*. New York: Henry Holt, 2016.

Chapter Twelve: COWORKERS

On Natalie Goldowski, please see the following sources:

Brown, Anthony Cave, and Charles B. MacDonald. *The Secret History of the Atomic Bomb*. New York: Dial, 1977.

Compton, Arthur Holly. *The Atomic Quest*. New York: Oxford University Press, 1956.

Gosling, F. G. *The Manhattan Project: Science in the Second World War*. Energy History Series. Washington, DC: US Department of Energy, 1990.

Howes, Ruth H., and Caroline L. Herzenberg. "Women of the Manhattan Project." *Technology Review* 96, no. 8 (1993): 32–40.

Libby, Leona Marshall. *The Uranium People.* New York: Crane, Russak, 1979.

Nichols, K. D. *The Road to Trinity.* New York: William Morrow, 1987.

Chapter Thirteen: THE REACTOR

For information on Joan Hinton and Los Alamos, J. Robert Oppenheimer's involvement there, Leona Woods's visit, the Technical Area, Enrico Fermi's arrival, the handling of the plutonium, and the incident Joan Hinton described, please refer to the following:

Fermi, Laura. *Atoms in the Family: My Life with Enrico Fermi.* Chicago: University of Chicago Press, 1954.

———. "The Fermis' Path to Los Alamos." In *Reminiscences of Los Alamos 1943–1945.* Edited by Lawrence Badash, Joseph O. Hirschfelder, and Herbert P. Broida. Studies in the History of Modern Science. Dordrecht, Netherlands, and Boston: D. Reidel, 1980.

Graf, William L. *Plutonium and the Rio Grande: Environmental Change and Contamination in the Nuclear Age.* New York: Oxford University Press, 1994.

Groves, Leslie R. *Now It Can Be Told: The Story of the Manhattan Project.* New York: Harper, 1962.

Hoddeson, Lillian, Paul W. Henriksen, Roger A. Meade, Catherine Westfall, Gordon Baym, Richard Hewlett, Alison Kerr, Robert Penneman, Leslie Redman, and Robert Seidel. *Critical Assembly: A Technical History of Los Alamos During the Oppenheimer Years, 1943–1945.* New York: Cambridge University Press, 1993.

Libby, Leona Marshall. *The Uranium People.* New York: Crane, Russak, 1979.

Shroyer, Jo Ann. *Secret Mesa: Inside Los Alamos National Laboratory.* New York: Wiley, 1997.

Ulam, S. M. *Adventures of a Mathematician.* New York: Charles Scribner's Sons, 1976.

Wilson, Jane S., and Charlotte Serber, eds. *Standing By and Making Do: Women of Wartime Los Alamos.* Los Alamos, NM: Los Alamos Historical Society, 1988.

Chapter Fourteen: DIZ

Information on Elizabeth "Diz" Graves and the Los Alamos site can be found in the following:

Bailey, Martha J. *American Women in Science: A Biographical Dictionary.* Denver: ABC-CLIO, 1994.

Groves, Leslie R. *Now It Can Be Told: The Story of the Manhattan Project.* New York: Harper, 1962.

Hoddeson, Lillian, Paul W. Henriksen, Roger A. Meade, Catherine Westfall, Gordon Baym, Richard Hewlett, Alison Kerr, Robert Penneman, Leslie Redman, and Robert Seidel. *Critical Assembly: A Technical History of Los Alamos During the Oppenheimer Years, 1943–1945.* New York: Cambridge University Press, 1993.

Lamont, Lansing. *Day of Trinity.* New York: Scribner, 1965.

Manley, Kathleen E. B. "Women of Los Alamos During World War II: Some of Their Views." *New Mexico Historical Review* (1990): 251–66.

Wilson, Jane S., and Charlotte Serber, eds. *Standing By and Making Do: Women of Wartime Los Alamos.* Los Alamos, NM: Los Alamos Historical Society, 1988.

Chapter Fifteen: THE PROFESSOR AND THE APPRENTICE

On Leona Woods, her relationship with Enrico Fermi and Fermi's wife, Laura, and the Chicago Met Lab, please refer to the following:

Compton, Arthur Holly. *Atomic Quest.* New York: Oxford
    University Press, 1956.
Fermi, Laura. *Atoms in the Family: My Life with Enrico Fermi.*
    Chicago: University of Chicago Press, 1954.
Folkart, Burt A. "Leona Marshall Libby Dies; Sole Woman to
    Work on Fermi's 1st Nuclear Reactor." *Los Angeles Times,*
    November 13, 1986.
Howes, Ruth H., and Caroline L. Herzenberg. "Women in
    Weapons Development: The Manhattan Project." In *Women
    and the Use of Military Force.* Edited by Ruth H. Howes and
    Michael R. Stevenson. Boulder, CO: Lynne Rienner, 1993.
Libby, Leona Marshall. *The Uranium People.* New York: Crane,
    Russak, 1979.
Nichols, K. D. *The Road to Trinity.* New York: William Morrow, 1987.

Chapter Sixteen: CHICAGO PILE-1

On Enrico Fermi, Leona Woods, the experiment beneath the
University of Chicago stadium, the bottle of Chianti, Arthur
Compton's decision to test the pile at the university, and the
subsequent work in the Argonne Forest and at the Hanford site,
please refer to the following:

Butler, Margaret, Caroline L. Herzenberg, and Jane Andrew.
    *Women in Scientific and Technical Positions at Argonne
    National Laboratory—Women and Argonne, Partners in
    Science: Five Decades of Memories and Meaning: 1946–1996.*
Compton, Arthur Holly. *Atomic Quest.* New York: Oxford
    University Press, 1956.
Fermi, Laura. *Atoms in the Family: My Life with Enrico Fermi.*
    Chicago: University of Chicago Press, 1954.
Gibson, Elizabeth. *Richland, Washington.* Images of America.
    Charleston, SC: Arcadia Publishing, 2002.
Greenbaum, Leonard. *A Special Interest: The Atomic Energy
    Commission, Argonne National Laboratory, and the Midwestern
    Universities.* Ann Arbor: University of Michigan Press, 1971.

Groves, Leslie R. *Now It Can Be Told: The Story of the Manhattan Project*. New York: Harper, 1962.
Libby, Leona Marshall. *The Uranium People*. New York: Crane, Russak, 1979.
Toomey, Elizabeth. *The Manhattan Project at Hanford Site*. Images of America. Charleston, SC: Arcadia Publishing, 2015.

Chapter Seventeen: THE LOS ALAMOS VISIT

On Maria Goeppert-Mayer's visit to Los Alamos and her ambiguous feelings about building the bomb, the following have been helpful:

Conant, Jennet. *109 East Palace: Robert Oppenheimer and the Secret City of Los Alamos*. New York: Simon & Schuster, 2005.
Dash, Joan. *A Life of One's Own: Three Gifted Women and the Men They Married*. New York: Harper & Row, 1973.
Ferry, Joseph P. *Maria Goeppert Mayer: Physicist*. Women in Science. Langhorne, PA: Chelsea House, 2003.
Gibson, Toni Michnovicz, and Jon Michnovicz. *Los Alamos: 1944–1947*. Images of America. Charleston, SC: Arcadia Publishing, 2005.
Hunner, Jon. *Inventing Los Alamos: The Growth of an Atomic Community*. Norman: University of Oklahoma Press, 2007.
Rempel, Trudy D. "Maria Gertrude Goeppert Mayer (1906–1972)." In *Women in Chemistry and Physics: A Biobibliographic Sourcebook*. Edited by Louise S. Grinstein, Rose K. Rose, and Miriam H. Rafailovich. Westport, CT: Greenwood Press, 1993.
Sachs, Robert G. "Maria Goeppert Mayer." In *Biographical Memoirs* 50, 310–28. National Academy of Sciences. Washington, DC: National Academies Press, 1979.
Wilson, Jane S., and Charlotte Serber, eds. *Standing By and Making Do: Women of Wartime Los Alamos*. Los Alamos, NM: Los Alamos Historical Society, 1988.

Chapter Eighteen: COMING TO AMERICA

On Elizabeth Rona's coming to America, Lise Meitner's memories, Rona's life in the United States, and the telegram she received from Brian O'Bryen, refer to the following:

Groueff, Stephane. *Manhattan Project: The Untold Story of the Making of the Atomic Bomb.* Boston: Little, Brown, 1967.

Hampel, Clifford A., ed. *The Encyclopedia of the Chemical Elements.* New York: Reinhold, 1968.

Parkinson, Claire L. *Breakthroughs: A Chronology of Great Achievements in Science and Mathematics, 1200–1930.* London: Mansell, 1985.

Rona, Elizabeth. *How It Came About: Radioactivity, Nuclear Physics, Atomic Energy.* Oak Ridge, TN: Oak Ridge Associated Universities, 1978.

Sime, Ruth Lewin. *Lise Meitner: A Life in Physics.* Berkeley: University of California Press, 1996.

Chapter Nineteen: TRINITY

On the Trinity test on July 16, 1945, there has been quite a lot of adult historical material written. Please refer to the following texts, as they have been the most helpful:

Bird, Kai, and Martin J. Sherwin. *American Prometheus: The Triumph and Tragedy of J. Robert Oppenheimer.* New York: Vintage Books, 2006.

Fermi, Laura. "The Fermis' Path to Los Alamos." In *Reminiscences of Los Alamos 1943–1945.* Edited by Lawrence Badash, Joseph O. Hirschfelder, and Herbert P. Broida. Studies in the History of Modern Science. Dordrecht, Netherlands, and Boston: D. Reidel, 1980.

Gibson, Toni Michnovicz, and Jon Michnovicz. *Los Alamos: 1944–1947.* Images of America. Charleston, SC: Arcadia Publishing, 2005.

Groves, Leslie R. *Now It Can Be Told: The Story of the Manhattan Project.* New York: Harper, 1962.

Hunner, Jon. *Inventing Los Alamos: The Growth of an Atomic Community.* Norman: University of Oklahoma Press, 2007.

Lamont, Lansing. *Day of Trinity.* New York: Scribner, 1965.

Szasz, Ferenc Morton. *The Day the Sun Rose Twice.* Albuquerque: University of New Mexico Press, 1984.

Wilson, Jane, ed. *All in Our Time: The Reminiscences of Twelve Nuclear Pioneers.* Chicago: Bulletin of the Atomic Scientists, 1975.

Chapter Twenty: THE END AND THE BEGINNING

Numerous works for an adult audience have been published on the bombing of Hiroshima and Nagasaki, and how it came to be. For additional information, refer to the following:

Bird, Kai, and Martin J. Sherwin. *American Prometheus: The Triumph and Tragedy of J. Robert Oppenheimer.* New York: Vintage Books, 2006.

Compton, Arthur Holly. *Atomic Quest.* New York: Oxford University Press, 1965.

Einstein, Albert. *Out of My Later Years: The Scientist, Philosopher, and Man Portrayed Through His Own Words.* New York: Philosophical Library, 1950.

Gosling, F. G. *The Manhattan Project: Science in the Second World War.* Energy History Series. Washington, DC: US Department of Energy, 1990.

Groueff, Stephane. *Manhattan Project: The Untold Story of the Atomic Bomb.* Boston: Little, Brown, 1967.

Groves, Leslie R. *Now It Can Be Told: The Story of the Manhattan Project.* New York: Harper, 1962.

Libby, Leona Marshall. *The Uranium People.* New York: Crane, Russak, 1979.

Rhodes, Richard. *The Making of the Atomic Bomb.* New York: Simon & Schuster, 1986.

Rona, Elizabeth. *How It Came About: Radioactivity, Nuclear Physics, Atomic Energy.* Oak Ridge, TN: Oak Ridge Associated Universities, 1978.

Taton, René, ed. *History of Science: Science in the Twentieth Century.* Translated by A. J. Pomerans. New York: Basic Books, 1964.

BIBLIOGRAPHY

Bernal, J. D. *Science in History.* London: Watts & Co., 1954.

Bigland, Eileen. *Madame Curie.* New York: Criterion, 1957.

Bird, Kai, and Martin J. Sherwin. *American Prometheus: The Triumph and Tragedy of J. Robert Oppenheimer.* New York: Vintage Books, 2006.

Compton, Arthur Holly. *Atomic Quest.* New York: Oxford University Press, 1956.

Crawford, Deborah. *Lise Meitner, Atomic Pioneer.* New York: Crown, 1969.

Conant, Jennet. *109 East Palace: Robert Oppenheimer and the Secret City of Los Alamos.* New York: Simon & Schuster, 2006.

Curie, Ève. *Madame Curie: A Biography.* Boston: Da Capo, 2001.

Dash, Joan. *A Life of One's Own: Three Gifted Women and the Men They Married.* New York: Harper & Row, 1973.

Einstein, Albert. *Out of My Later Years: The Scientist, Philosopher, and Man Portrayed Through His Own Words.* New York: Philosophical Library, 1950.

Emling, Shelley. *Marie Curie and Her Daughters: The Private Lives of Science's First Family.* New York: St. Martin's/Griffin, 2013.

Fermi, Laura. *Atoms in the Family: My Life with Enrico Fermi.* Chicago: University of Chicago Press, 1995.

Ferry, Joseph P. *Maria Goeppert Mayer: Physicist.* Women in Science. Langhorne, PA: Chelsea House, 2003.

Frisch, Otto Robert. *What Little I Remember.* Cambridge, UK: Cambridge University Press, 1979.

Gibson, Elizabeth. *Richland, Washington.* Images of America. Charleston, SC: Arcadia Publishing, 2002.

Gibson, Toni Michnovicz, and Jon Michnovicz. *Los Alamos: 1944–1947.* Images of America. Arcadia Publishing, 2005.

Giroud, Françoise. *Marie Curie: A Life.* Translated by Lydia Davis. New York: Holmes and Meier, 1986.

Goldsmith, Barbara. *Obsessive Genius: The Inner World of Marie Curie.* New York: W. W. Norton, 2005.

Graff, William L. *Plutonium and the Rio Grande: Environmental Change and Contamination in the Nuclear Age.* New York: Oxford University Press, 1994.

Groueff, Stephane. *Manhattan Project: The Untold Story of the Making of the Atomic Bomb.* Boston: Little, Brown, 1967.

Groves, Leslie. *Now It Can Be Told: The Story of the Manhattan Project.* New York: Harper, 1962.

Hahn, Otto. *Otto Hahn: A Scientific Autobiography.* New York: Charles Scribner's Sons, 1966.

Hawkins, David, Edith C. Truslow, and Ralph Carlisle Smith. *Project Y: The Los Alamos Story.* Part I, *Toward Trinity,* and Part II, *Beyond Trinity.* The History of Modern Physics, 1800–1950, Vol. 2. Los Angeles: Tomash Publishers, 1983.

Hoddeson, Lillian, Paul W. Henriksen, Roger A. Meade, Catherine Westfall, Gordon Baym, Richard Hewlett, Alison Kerr, Robert Penneman, Leslie Redman, and Robert Seidel. *Critical Assembly: A Technical History of Los Alamos During the Oppenheimer Years, 1943–1945.* New York: Cambridge University Press, 1993.

Hoffmann, Klaus. *Otto Hahn: Achievement and Responsibility.* New York: Springer-Verlag, 2001.

Hunner, Jon. *Inventing Los Alamos: The Growth of an Atomic Community.* Norman: University of Oklahoma Press, 2007.

Kelly, Cynthia C. *Manhattan Project: The Birth of the Atomic Bomb in the Words of Its Creators, Eyewitnesses, and Historians.* New York: Black Dog & Leventhal, 2009.

Kunetka, James. *The General and the Genius: Groves and Oppenheimer—the Unlikely Partnership That Built the Atom Bomb.* Washington, DC: Regnery, 2015.

Lanouette, William. *Genius in the Shadows: A Biography of Leo Szilard, the Man Behind the Bomb.* New York: Skyhorse, 2013.

Lawren, William. *The General and the Bomb: A Biography of General Leslie R. Groves, Director of the Manhattan Project.* New York: Dodd Mead, 1988.

Libby, Leona Marshall. *The Uranium People.* New York: Crane, Russak, 1979.

Nichols, K. D. *The Road to Trinity.* New York: William Morrow, 1987.

Opfell, Olga. "Triumph and Rebuff: Irène Joliot-Curie." In *The Lady Laureates: Women Who Have Won the Nobel Prize.* Metuchen, NJ: Scarecrow Press, 1986.

Rempel, Trudy D. "Maria Gertrude Goeppert Mayer (1906–1972)." In *Women in Chemistry and Physics: A Biobibliographic Sourcebook.* Edited by Louise S. Grinstein, Rose K. Rose, and Miriam H. Rafailovich. Westport, CT: Greenwood Press, 1993.

Rhodes, Richard. *The Making of the Atomic Bomb.* New York: Simon & Schuster, 1986.

Rife, Patricia. *Lise Meitner and the Dawn of the Nuclear Age.* Boston: Birkhäuser, 2006.

Rona, Elizabeth. *How It Came About: Radioactivity, Nuclear Physics, Atomic Energy.* Oak Ridge, TN: Oak Ridge Associated Universities, 1978.

Schwartz, David N. *The Last Man Who Knew Everything: The Life and Times of Enrico Fermi, Father of the Nuclear Age.* New York: Basic Books, 2017.

Segrè, Gino, and Bettina Hoerlin. *The Pope of Physics: Enrico Fermi and the Birth of the Atomic Age.* New York: Henry Holt, 2016.

Shroyer, Jo Ann. *Secret Mesa: Inside Los Alamos National Laboratory.* New York: Wiley, 1997.

Sime, Ruth Lewin. "Lise Meitner and the Discovery of Fission." *Journal of Chemical Education* 66 (1989): 373–75.

———. *Lise Meitner: A Life in Physics.* Berkeley: University of California Press, 1997.

Taton, René, ed. *History of Science: Science in the Twentieth Century.* Translated by A. J. Pomerans. New York: Basic Books, 1966.

Toomey, Elizabeth. *The Manhattan Project at Hanford Site.* Images of America. Charleston, SC: Arcadia Publishing, 2015.

Ulam, S. M. *Adventures of a Mathematician.* New York: Charles Scribner's Sons, 1976.

US Government, Los Alamos Scientific Laboratory. *Project Y: The Los Alamos Project—Manhattan District History, the Development of the First Atomic Bomb, Trinity, Alberta Project, Tinian, Plutonium, Uranium, Experiments, Physics and Explosives.* Progressive Management, 2017.

Watkins, Sallie A. "Lise Meitner (1878–1968)." In *Women in Chemistry and Physics: A Biobibliographic Sourcebook.* Edited by Louise S. Grinstein, Rose K. Rose, and Miriam H. Rafailovich. Westport, CT: Greenwood Press, 1993.

Weeks, Mary Elvira. *Discovery of the Elements.* 6th ed. Easton, PA: Journal of Chemical Education, 1956.

Westcott, Ed. *Oak Ridge.* Images of America. Charleston, SC: Arcadia Publishing, 2005.

Wilson, Jane, ed. *All in Our Time: The Reminiscences of Twelve Nuclear Pioneers.* Chicago: Bulletin of the Atomic Scientists, 1975.

Wilson, Jane S., and Charlotte Serber, eds. *Standing By and Making Do: Women of Wartime Los Alamos.* Los Alamos, NM: Los Alamos Historical Society, 2008.

ASSOCIATIONS, ARCHIVES, AND LIBRARIES

American Museum of Science and Energy, Oak Ridge, TN
Atomic Heritage Foundation, Washington, DC
B Reactor Museum Association, Richland, WA
Bradbury Science Museum, Los Alamos, NM
Department of Energy: The Manhattan Project
L'association Curie et Joliot-Curie, Paris

BIBLIOGRAPHY

Library of Congress, Washington, DC
Los Alamos Historical Society, Los Alamos, NM
National Museum of Nuclear Science and History, Albuquerque, NM
Smithsonian Institution Archives, Washington, DC
Wellcome Library, London

INDEX

A

Advisory Committee on Uranium, 88–89, 129, 233
aluminum, 50, 54–55, 139
American Physical Society, 193
Anderson, Herbert, 132, 165
Anschluss (annexation of Austria), 71
anti-feminine bias. *See* Sexism
anti-Semitism, 66–67, 69–71
Argonne Forest, 170–71, 176–77
Army Corps of Engineers, 106–7
artificial radioactivity, 52–55, 56, 65
atomic bombardment, 168–69, 232
atomic bombing of Hiroshima and Nagasaki, 209–16, *225–26*, 236
attack on Pearl Harbor, 90, 128, 129, 208, 234
Austro-Hungarian Army, 188–89

B

Bardeen, John, 142
barium, 74, 76
Battle of France, 208
Battle of Iwo Jima, 235
Becquerel, Henri, 18, 20–21, 231
beta decay, 35, 55, 91
bismuth-210, 48
Bohr, Niels, 54, 141
    Lise Meitner and, 60–61, 71–72

nuclear fission, 77, 79–81
Solvay Conference (1933), 53
Washington Conference (1939), 80–81, 84, 95, 232
Boltzmann, Ludwig, 29–30, 31–33
Boole, George, 126
Boolean algebra, 126
Born, Max, 99–103, 115–16, 185–86
Bredig, Georg, 39–40
Bredig, Rosa, 39
Bremen, SS, 118
Brillouin zones, 128

C

cadmium, 172, 175–76
California Institute of Technology (Caltech), 103
Cambridge University, 97
Carnegie Institution for Science, 89
Catholic University of America, 193
Chadwick, James, 231
Chamié, Catherine, 49
Chicago Pile-1, 140, 170–77, 200
Civil Service Law (Germany), 69–70
Columbia River, 177–78, 179
Columbia University, 81–82, 89, 118–20, 129–30, 132, 141, 167, 194–95, 234